24 FILMS THAT MATTER

American Cinema – Then To Now

KEN WHITE

PEARSON

Custom
Publishing

Printed in the United States of America

10 9 8 7 6 5 4 3

ISBN 0-536-36347-1

2006420374

JK/SD

Please visit our web site at *www.pearsoncustom.com*

PEARSON CUSTOM PUBLISHING
75 Arlington Street, Suite 300, Boston, MA 02116
A Pearson Education Company

CONTENTS

Preface . . . . *ix*

First Images . . . . *xi*

Chapter 1   THE BEGINNING
            A TRIP TO THE MOON* AND *THE GREAT TRAIN ROBBERY **1**

A Trip to the Moon   3

The Great Train Robbery   5

Analysis.   5

Film Theaters   6

Film Language.   6

Trivia.   7

Chapter 2   D. W. GRIFFITH
            THE BIRTH OF A NATION **9**

Feature Film—1914   12

Birth of the Studio System   13

D. W. Griffith   14

Trivia.   15

Chapter 3   CHAPLIN
            CITY LIGHTS **17**

Buster Keaton.   21

Harold Lloyd.   21

City Lights   22

Feature Films   22

The Silent Frame 23
Trivia 24

Chapter 4   THE SILENT ERA
         THE CROWD **25**

The Crowd 27
A Different Art Form 28
The Coming of Sound 28
Moving Pictures 29
Audiences 30
Sound 30
Trivia 31

Chapter 5   THE COMING OF SOUND
         SCARFACE **33**

The Loss 35
The Gain 36
Scarface 36
Censorship 37
Censorship and the Coming of Sound 38
The Production Code 39
Howard Hawks 40
Trivia 41

Chapter 6   PRE-CODE FILMS
         RED DUST **AND** *TROUBLE IN PARADISE* **43**

Red Dust 46
Trouble in Paradise 47
Ernst Lubitsch 48
Trivia 48

Chapter 7   SCREWBALL COMEDY
         IT HAPPENED ONE NIGHT **49**

Charm of Screwball Comedy 52
Class and Screwball Comedy 52
Marriage and Comedy 53
Dialogue 1930s 53

Frank Capra 54
Trivia 54

Chapter 8   WESTERNS
              STAGECOACH **55**
End of the Western 57
The Roots 58
Stagecoach 58
Road Picture 59
Mise-En-Scene 59
John Wayne 60
John Ford 60
Trivia 61

Chapter 9   HOLLYWOOD REBEL
              CITIZEN KANE **63**
Influences 65
Future Filmmakers 67
Controversy 68
Welles 68
Trivia 70

Chapter 10   THE STUDIO SYSTEM
               CASABLANCA **71**
Hollywood Studio System 73
History 76
Character Ramp 76
Trivia 77

Chapter 11   GENRE
               THE PALM BEACH STORY **79**
Genre 81
The Palm Beach Story 82
Preston Sturges 83
End of the Genre 83

Chapter 12   **FILM NOIR**
         DOUBLE INDEMNITY **85**

The Roots 87
Billy Wilder 90
Noir Today 91
Trivia 91

Chapter 13   **BLACKLISTING**
         THE FRONT **93**

Cold War/Blacklisting 95
Blacklisting 97
The Front 98
The Coming of Television 98
Trivia 100

Chapter 14   **THE 1950s**
         ON THE WATERFRONT **101**

Structure 104
Method Acting 105
Brando 105
Kazan 106
Trivia 106

Chapter 15   **CLASSICAL HOLLYWOOD STYLE**
         REAR WINDOW **107**

Hitchcock 109
Rear Window 111
Trivia 113

Chapter 16   **SEX IN THE 1950s**
         PILLOW TALK **115**

Analysis 117
1959 118
The Influence of European Trends—1959 118
Actors in the 50s 118
Trivia 119

Chapter 17   1960s
                     THE GRADUATE **121**
Death of the Production Code 123
Blacklisting Fades Away 124
The Hollywood Studios. 124
The Graduate 125
French New Wave 127

Chapter 18   VIOLENCE 60s STYLE
                     BONNIE AND CLYDE **129**
1960s. 131
New Heroes 132
Box Office Trends 132
Trivia 133

Chapter 19   1970s
                     THE GODFATHER **135**
The Godfather. 138
Trivia 140

Chapter 20   CORPORATE HOLLYWOOD
                     STAR WARS **141**
The Independents. 144
Corporate Hollywood 144
Trivia. 145

Chapter 21   FILM SCHOOL
                     BOYZ N THE HOOD **147**
Minorities/Women in Hollywood 149
Film School. 150
Women 151
Minorities 151
Boyz N The Hood 152
John Singleton 152
African American 153
Asian 153

Latino/Latina 154
Today 154
Trivia 154

Chapter 22   HOLLYWOOD TODAY
            CRASH **155**
Film Festivals 159
Crash 159
Trivia 160

Afterwards *161*
Recommended Films 162

PREFACE

There are a number of central ideas that shape the content of this book. First and foremost, this book is designed to be read in conjunction with watching the movie that forms the basis of each chapter. Each movie can be watched before or after; it makes little difference. I have tried very hard to make sure that nothing I have written will fundamentally alter the viewing experience. If you watch a movie before reading a chapter, there will be added background and flavor. If you watch a film afterwards, different elements may take on more significance. Ultimately, my goal is to enrich your understanding and appreciation of the films and Hollywood without interfering with the pure enjoyment that each film offers.

At times, I provide social context and historical background to give you some sense of how a film might have seemed to audiences when it first appeared. After all, gossip, social trends, and politics have always combined to provide context for film. It was true in 1910; it is true today.

This is not a book of analysis, critique or criticism. Most movies are designed to be self-contained blocks of entertainment with no need of outside augmentation. Audiences have always gone to the movies to be entertained, and with little preparation. Ultimately movies are simple storytelling vehicles that work or do not work for audiences no matter the intent of the filmmakers or the underlying themes and meaning.

I have also purposely refused to use one film as a means of explaining a different film. I understand the dilemma, but to me if you have not seen the film or don't know the director, all references—no matter how insightful—are worthless.

The chapters are organized in a chronological order, but there is no requirement to read them one after the other in a linear fashion. If your mood is for a romantic comedy, read those chapters and watch those movies. If you are in the mood for romantic suspense, skip to Hitchcock; a western, watch *Stagecoach*; in a more intellectual mood, watch *Citizen Kane*.

The chapter topics and films were chosen based on several narrow criteria, but the overall narrative thread of the book is basically how and why Hollywood made the films it did and does.

The specific films and directors were chosen based on the simple question of which directors and which films influenced the directors and films that followed—not just for a few years, but decade after decade.

Since 1900 more than 50,000 films have been made just in America. For most of that period, Hollywood has dominated the world of film making. I have chosen to concentrate only on Hollywood films and have chosen just 24 films to tell the story. This seems a manageable number of films to watch but obviously much was ignored and omitted.

I have skipped genres like the musical, the war film and horror. The musical as a genre has faded away. The war film is still with us but has not greatly influenced other filmmakers or audiences. Horror is not to my taste though it has a substantial and honorable role in the history of film. Animation, Disney, Pixar and the new technologies deserve a book of their own.

Great directors from Martin Scorsese and Steven Spielberg to William Wyler and George Cuckor have been omitted, not because they did not make great films and not because they did not make popular films, but because their visions were unique and uncopiable. They may have inspired the next generation of directors to make films, but their voices were their own.

Trivia was added to give flavor and context because it is often the minute details that humanize. Film, because of its very nature, can be seen to be this grandly-conceived work of art that springs whole from the writer and director. But many times great, influential films are just a collection of happy coincidences and a serendipity of good fortune. The trivia came from many sources but most was verified through the international movie database.

In some ways, this book has tried to combine contradictory goals. The view is focused on Hollywood and a few films, but the intent is to give a broad understanding of how Hollywood films work for audiences around the world. These 24 films are a good start.

Ken White

FIRST IMAGES

Once pioneers, inventors and visionaries had developed useful motion picture cameras, film stock and projectors, the question was: what next? How could one make money taking moving pictures? Was the motion picture a novelty? Or a freak of human physiology that produced interesting effects but was really an unimportant toy? Of course a movie camera could answer scientific questions such as how do birds fly or how many hooves on a horse touch the ground simultaneously when they gallop, but not much money was to be made taking pictures of horses and birds.

The answers took a while to figure out since the invention of movie cameras did not lead logically and immediately to feature films. Other inventions from the same era had become consumer items. Cameras and film for still photography were sold to mass audiences once the cameras became cheap and simple enough. But movie cameras were still much too expensive, cumbersome and complex for a mass audience. It would be almost 50 years before 8 millimeter cameras become possible for a mass audience and almost 100 years for a new technology—camcorders, video tape and television—to make home movies easy and cheap.

In many ways the movie camera would seem to be similar to the phonograph (invented roughly 15 years before film). Both seemed to capture reality and play it back. But unlike music on records, movies are not just reality played back. Feature film is not just a faithful recording of a staged production—live theater captured on film. Movies fundamentally alter time and reality to create a new reality. It is an illusionary reality that—through a combination of editing, camera position, framing and many other factors—creates a reality that never existed.

At first, filmmakers tried capturing and selling faithful recordings of everyday events. First films are literally mundane events like a train pulling into a train station, a couple kissing or a famous hootchy-kootchy dancer, little Sheba from the Chicago world's fair. These are novelties that people would pay a small sum to see a few times, but with little long-term potential. It is easy to see that it is just not possible to make money showing trains coming into a train station.

The future of movie pictures was not capturing reality like the phonograph or still camera, but telling stories that enthralled, excited and touched the hearts of audiences. Surprisingly, movie pictures turned out to be much more like the novel than anything else. Like the printed word on a page, film was not bound by the physical realities of the world. Ultimately, the stories told by feature films were limited only by the imagination and cleverness of the filmmaker. Anything that could be conceived and shot could be brought to the screen unbound by the laws of physics.

It is not surprising that it took the first filmmakers a while to develop the language and stories of film. The process was simple. Many people tried many different things, and those that audiences liked and for which they were willing to pay money were remade. Over and over again this process of trying something and letting the box office decide ultimately produced what we know as feature film. It is a process that shaped Hollywood and continues today.

CHAPTER 1

THE BEGINNING

A Trip to the Moon and
The Great Train Robbery

Courtesy of Bettman/Corbis.

Courtesy of the John Springer Collection/Corbis.

By 1900 moving images had been around for more than 20 years. They had gone from being a technological novelty to an everyday experience readily available in major urban areas. But film was still young and the future uncertain. This was long before feature films, before stars and Hollywood. The year 1900 was long before anyone had an idea what film should or could be. Many of the technical sides of shooting and projecting film had been refined. But the artistic, storytelling and business side had yet to gel.

Two good examples of the best in film in these early years are *A Trip to the Moon* (1902) and *The Great Train Robbery* (1903). The style of one film leads to an artistic and commercial dead end. The other becomes the template for film that continues today.

A TRIP TO THE MOON

At the turn of the century, films like *A Trip to the Moon* were immensely popular. Urban audiences with a little extra money and leisure time were willing to pay modest sums to be entertained by fanciful, amusing productions. In *A Trip to the Moon*, all manner of fantastic events take place. Alien creatures explode and disappear, the stars of the sky are beautiful women, and all it takes to reach the moon is the proper cannon. The film was fun; it is still fun today. But it lacks much of what we now expect from movies. There is no central protagonist, no star, no romance, no drama and perhaps more crucially, no emotional connection by the audience with the characters on the screen.

Méliès

The creator of *A Trip to the Moon* and one of the leading directors of the time was George Méliès. It is easy to see from his films that he was originally a magician. Film has a wonderful ability to manipulate time and space—to make things appear and disappear, to reshape reality, to condense time and space. Méliès' films were very popular, yet by the middle of the next decade he would be selling trinkets, toys and candy at a kiosk in a Paris train station.

The early film business was a tough competitive business. Rivals copied his style, undercut his prices and pirated his films. Competitors like Pathe and Gaumont were better organized and more effective distributors than Méliès. But most importantly, Méliès never grew as a film maker. He was one of the first to think of film as a series of scenes. Most of the early films were just one scene from one camera position. Everything happened in one time, one place, from beginning to end. Méliès' films moved from one scene to the next scene with a sense of the progression of time. But he never went further. There is no cutting, no editing in any of his films except to produce his visual special effects. There is no cutting back and forth from one scene to another to give a sense of continuity or connection, no cutting from wide to tight to medium frames inside a scene. Méliès never moved the camera, never varied the camera position or angle. That was not his interest. He saw film through the eyes of a magician.

As others developed new ways of telling a story, his films no longer touched the audience. Amazement without emotional content was not the future of film. He made more than 500 films, all shorts or one reelers, none longer than 15 minutes. Most of his films have disappeared. The prints were recycled to salvage the silver and to make boot heels out of the celluloid. About 150 of his films survive.

Méliès and other leading makers of these kinds of short whimsical films were often French. French films from this era tended to have high production values and used film in a playful, amusing style with lots of camera tricks and special effects.

From the beginning, film was international. Since film was without dialogue, the country of origin did not matter. Title cards could be easily and cheaply inserted into any film for distribution in any country. Many of the original inventors, distributors and directors of film were French. The Lumiere Brothers Auguste and Louis, Charles Pathe, Léon Gaumont and of course Méliès all had a significant impact on the development of film. With the coming of World War I, France's position as one of the leading makers of film in the world ended. With America's leading competitor now gone, Hollywood would begin its dominance of film that continues today.

While the French were known for elegant, playful films that incorporated significant special effects, American films tended to be plot-driven melodramas with chases, fights and shootouts or slapstick comedy as the main attraction. One of the best and most influential of these early films is *The Great Train Robbery*, one of the first block-buster hits in the industry.

THE GREAT TRAIN ROBBERY

There are easy comparisons to be made between *The Great Train Robbery* and *A Trip to the Moon*. Special effects in *The Great Train Robbery* are there as part of the story. The rear projection in the train car scene was done to create a sense of reality. The illusion is part of the story. The audience might not even be aware that there are special effects at all. In the same vein, the tossing of a dummy from the moving train to create the illusion that the train engineer has been murdered is there because it is an integral part of the story. This scene establishes that the train robbers are ruthless bad guys and deserve to be shot to death at the climax of the film.

Special effects in *A Trip to the Moon* are there for amusement. Acrobatic aliens in *A Trip to the Moon* explode for no real storytelling purpose. The film is a visual magic show full of cleverness and humor, but lacks the narrative thread that audiences will ultimately decide should be an integral element of film.

In *The Great Train Robbery,* however, pragmatism is the rule. The camera moves because it is on a train. Riders on horseback come toward the camera moving from wide shot to close up, increasing the dramatic impact of the images. The camera pans to keep the robbers in frame. In every scene in *The Great Train Robbery* the camera is subservient to the action in the frame. In *A Trip to the Moon*, the camera is there not to tell the story but in some sense to be the real star of the film. The visual effects are in essence the sole purpose of making the film.

ANALYSIS

In 1900 no one knew what the future of film would be. By 1910 it was clear. The future lay with story. Audiences preferred the kinds of stories typified by *The Great Train Robbery* to films like *A Trip to the Moon* that concentrated merely on the visual power of film. Of course film would communicate visually, but the story would also need to reach the audience on an emotional level. Audiences wanted to care about what happened to the characters on the screen. They wanted to feel their emotions, understand their motivations, be thrilled by their daring and learn from their actions.

Because audiences would determine the direction of film at the box office, it is important to note that the future of film would not belong to any of the pioneer directors or inventors. Thomas A. Edison, Méliès, the Lumiere brothers and all of the other early pioneers did not make the transition to feature film. The future of film would be shaped and dominated by the men who knew what audiences wanted: the owners of the first film theaters, the Nickelodeons.

FILM THEATERS

The first film theaters were most often just rented store fronts. There might be a piano player for music, benches to sit on, a white screen, and not much else. The entertainment usually was roughly an hour's worth of short films shown one after the other. The offerings changed regularly. Admission price was a nickel, hence the name Nickelodeons. These Nickelodeons grew rapidly, and just as rapidly were replaced by theaters built specifically for films. In 1900 there were no Nickelodeons; by 1905, they dominated; by 1910 they were gone.

Men who started as owners of Nickelodeons would, over the next decade, become the Hollywood tycoons. Men with names like Fox, Goldwyn, and Mayer would determine the course of film. Geniuses and stars would come and go. Directors and writers could become hot or cold, but theater owners needed a consistent series of audience-pleasing films. Theater owners became the makers of film to make sure that their theaters had a continual supply of movies audiences wanted to see. They were not directors or writers or camera people. But they knew what audiences wanted and they hired the talent to make films to please their audience.

In 1910 no one knew where film was headed. Stars were a new wrinkle and feature films were yet to be offered, but the basics were in place. The early innovators had developed the equipment and the visual language of film. In 1910 Hollywood was still just a place to grow oranges. By 1920 Hollywood would dominate world film making. Yet in 1910 no one could see it coming. By 1910 the language of film was ready to communicate to mass audiences, but the business of film that we know today was still over the horizon. There was no Hollywood and feature films were not even an idea waiting in the wings.

FILM LANGUAGE

In these first formative years the visual content and presentation of film moved dramatically. Bit by bit, lesson by lesson, filmmakers quickly invented film language. By 1910, editing for pacing to connect related actions happening simultaneously in different places and for emphasis was well established. The repertoire of shot selection was well defined as well. Wide shots to show you where you are, medium shots for character interaction, and close-ups for punctuation and visual impact have become standardized. It is the same visual language we use today.

TRIVIA

The Great Train Robbery was shot in New Jersey by the Edison Company. The film took in more money than any other film until 1912 and sparked a surge in westerns that lasted until the 1970s.

Edwin Porter, director of *The Great Train Robbery,* directed a number of other notable films for the Edison Company, but none was better or more influential. By the middle of the next decade, he was no longer directing films, but instead was concentrating his effort on technical improvements for cameras and projectors.

The hammish actor who played the tenderfoot dancer and the railroad passenger shot by the bandits went on to become the first cowboy hero western star, Bronco Billy. He made hundreds of films. One of his fans was a Viennese woman who named her son Billy after her hero. Billy Wilder would later become one of the great film directors of Hollywood during the 1940s and 50s.

C H A P T E R   2

D. W. GRIFFITH

The Birth of a Nation

Courtesy of Bettman/Corbis.

D.W. Griffith is probably the single most influential filmmaker of the silent era. Not that he was always first or the most innovative, but he was a strong, continual presence in this crucial formative period. His career spanned from near the beginning of film to after the coming of sound. He was one of the few who grew and evolved with the medium. A contemporary of Méliès and Porter, he started by making simple, crude one reelers. He finished making some of the great feature films of the silent era long after most other pioneers had disappeared from filmmaking.

A perfectionist and innovator, Griffith continually strove to develop ways to improve his storytelling techniques in all facets of filmmaking. Consequently, his films impacted everything from acting and narrative structure to lighting and editing, and helped shape what became feature film. Of all the silent films, none was more influential than his first masterpiece, *The Birth of a Nation*. Yet it is impossible to discuss *The Birth of a Nation* and Griffith's career without acknowledging a huge and disturbing flaw in this first masterpiece of American film.

The problem with *The Birth of a Nation* is simply that it told the story of the Civil War from a southern perspective. The heroes of the film are the Ku Klux Klan. The imagery of white hooded Ku Klux Klan members riding to the rescue of beleaguered plantation owners is dramatic, great cinema, yet is politically and morally repugnant and difficult to watch today. But there is no denying that the business of making movies changed almost overnight with this one film. It changed in America and it changed around the world.

FEATURE FILM—1914

By 1910, the idea of feature films was in the air, but no one was quite sure of form, content, or who the audience would be. Before 1914, feature film tended to be of two varieties, either faithful filming of stage productions, usually with famous actors, or historical spectacles with magnificent sets and epic stories.

Films of stage productions generally were shot as static wide shots with no camera movement or editing. The attraction was to see famous stage actors in well-known productions. They were popular and proved that audiences would watch feature length film, but they were a visual dead end. Painted back drops, stage acting and a static camera without editing to establish tempo would not be the future of film.

Epic large-scale productions with huge casts and mammoth, spectacular sets also were popular. Produced mostly in Italy, they tended to be grand in scale yet slow and ponderous in tempo. Again, the stories tended to be told in wide, long master shots with little editing or camera movement. *Quo Vadis* (1914 Italy), for instance, more than two hours in length, had fewer than sixty shots and no close-ups.

The Birth of a Nation provided a blueprint for what feature film should be. It mixed large scale epic storytelling with intimate, touching romance. There is danger and death as well as love and hope. There are large-scale battles, rides to the rescue, numerous action skirmishes, tension, suspense, humor, and separated lovers, all blended together on a human scale with which audiences could identify. The characters in the film had depth and personality. The actors were not two-dimensional caricatures, but flesh and blood creations with needs and wants that the audience could understand and root for. The acting itself was often subtle and nuanced.

The visuals are also substantially different from most previous features. Everything in *The Birth of a Nation* had been done before, but never on this scale. The camera moved. It raced across the battlefield with the soldiers, rode to the rescue with the Ku Klux Klan, and yet tenderly caught the complicated affections of parting lovers. There are intimate close-ups of worried parents intercut with dramatic wide shots of grand battles involving cannons, cavalry and hundreds of soldiers. The film moves. There are almost 1,400 shots in the film. The total effect was quite different from anything done before. So were the profits.

By the standards of 1914, *The Birth of a Nation* had a huge budget, around a hundred thousand dollars, but it took in more than a million dollars in the first six months of its release. The film was wildly popular and cut across class boundaries. It played in Nickelodeons and the best live theaters in the country. It was hugely popular in America and around the world. After *The Birth of a Nation* it was clear that there was a lot of money to be made in feature films.

But it was just as obvious that the way *The Birth of a Nation* had been produced was not sustainable. D. W. Griffith had used his own money, borrowing from anyone he could, while most actors worked based on his personal promise of being paid after the film was released. This is the model for making independent films then and now, but it is no way to run a business or a movie studio.

BIRTH OF THE STUDIO SYSTEM

Though they seem very similar, the business of making one-reelers is quite different from the business of making feature films. The capital requirements for making one-reelers are modest. The cost of making features is enormous. There were many companies making one-reel films. Few would make feature films. For one-reelers to make a profit distribution did not have to be widespread. Distribution for features would be worldwide.

One-reelers often were shot in just a day or two and were literally in the Nickelodeons the next week. Cash flow was not a problem. Managing small companies like this was relatively easy and uncomplicated. The stories were simple enough that there was no need for elaborate sets or costumes. A small group of actors with a director and cameraman could literally crank out a film in a few days for just the cost of salaries and film.

Feature films are quite different. Distribution needs to be global to recoup the substantial costs. There can be long delays between the start of film making and the return of box office proceeds. Features need highly-skilled individuals in a number of areas like writing, directing, camera, costume, set design, editing, accounting, marketing, legal, distribution, and advertising.

Feature films were not only more expensive, complicated and time-consuming but inherently more risky. The companies making good money producing short films had little interest or incentive to make features. Why take the risk when they were doing quite well making one-reelers?

There were other problems. The audiences for one-reelers tended to be quite different from those for feature films. A series of shorts playing in a Nickelodeon attracted mostly working- and lower-class audiences. Most feature films to this point were prestige projects that attracted a middle- to upper-class audience. Often these films played in the same theater as live theatrical productions and cost substantially more than the collection of one-reelers at a Nickelodeon.

The Birth of A Nation showed that with the right story and visuals, feature film could attract huge audiences of all classes around the world and generate tremendous profits. There were risks, of course, but the rewards made it at all worthwhile.

By 1920 a few studios in Hollywood were the dominant film making companies in the world. Often they took in more than 70 percent of world box office proceeds in a single year. The structure of each of the major Hollywood studios was similar. They owned chains of theaters across the country to guarantee that the films they produced would reach an audience. They had offices in the major capitals of the world to make sure that their films were properly distributed internationally. Each studio had offices in New York to ensure a steady stream of investment capital. Major stars, writers, directors, cinematographers, editors, and other major players were under exclusive contracts to make sure that there was the talent available to produce a steady flow of new films.

Hollywood quickly learned that with so much money at risk, the stars were a useful means of insuring profits and promoting new films. Hollywood also learned that some stories could be told again and again. Repackaging and reworking these audience-pleasing genres became a staple of Hollywood filmmaking. Genres and stars help define Hollywood films. The formula has not changed much in the last 90 years.

In 1910, features didn't exist. By 1920, they dominated the movie business. In 1910, Hollywood was mostly orange groves. By 1920, Hollywood was the glamour capital of the world. In 1910, Nickelodeons were common; by 1920 there were movie palaces in all the major cities devoted to showing the latest Hollywood creations. The film business had arrived. It would not change substantially until the mid 1960s. Sound would come and the silent films would go but the studio system was the way America made films for the next four decades.

D. W. GRIFFITH

Before he started directing movies, D. W. Griffith was basically a failure. He wanted to be a novelist but his writing was turgid and dense. He tried writing plays but again he was a failure. He tried acting but on stage and film he was stiff and hammish. Since he was a little older than most of the other early film actors, he was asked to direct. He had so little confidence in his directing ability that he made the production company promise that he could go back to acting if he were ill suited to directing. He never went back to acting.

Though he was a failure as a playwright and novelist, his understanding of basic storytelling technique and structure proved useful to his filmmaking. After all, silent film is just storytelling utilizing the new medium of cinematography to convey the story instead of written words and dialogue. A perfectionist, he learned and grew as he went along. Through trial and error, from film to film, he discovered how movies communicated. After making nearly 450 short films in eight years, he understood how to manipulate the audience with camera movement, shot selection and editing. He was ready to move from the confines of short films into longer, more complicated stories. He was ready to make the first masterpiece of American cinema, *The Birth of a Nation*.

Yet at this time of his greatest success, he was dogged by accusations that he was a racist. He would go on to make a number of other interesting and sometimes great films, but by 1931 he would be out of the business of making movies. Audiences changed; he could not. The values of the roaring twenties and the jazz age were incompatible with his formal Victorian sensibilities. By 1930, the coming of sound and the great depression would change audience preferences and Hollywood film making yet again. Griffith died in 1948, acknowledged as one of the great innovators of early cinema, yet for decades unable to make films in the Hollywood he helped create.

D. W. Griffith is just one of many great filmmakers whose vision and sensibilities matched the needs of the day, but who, when times changed, could not adapt and were left behind and forgotten. The business of making movies is ruthless. The ticket-buying public validates at the box office whether their wants, fantasies, ambition, and desires are being fulfilled. When the ability to satisfy an audience is gone, no reputation or technical prowess will cover the gap. Few directors can make great, audience-pleasing films decade after decade.

TRIVIA

There was no script for *The Birth of a Nation*. D. W. Griffith had the entire film organized in his head.

All of the scenes in the film were shot in one take, except for a minor scene that had to be shot a second time.

The Birth of a Nation was based on a novel "The Clansman," written by a friend of D. W. Griffith.

All the black characters in the film were played by white actors in black face, which was the standard of the time.

Many of the battle scenes, locations, military uniforms, poses and modes of dress were scrupulously copied from civil war era photographs.

Because of the huge demand for film prints, the original negative quickly wore out. All later copies of the film had to be made from release prints, reducing quality.

Because of the racist overtones of the movie, it was later banned in several major cities, including Los Angeles, and caused riots in Boston and other East Coast cities.

At the film's premiere, D. W. Griffith hired the entire Los Angeles Philharmonic to play the score for the film.

Each major character in the film had a particular musical theme.

C H A P T E R   3
CHAPLIN

City Lights

Courtesy of Bettman/Corbis.

Charlie Chaplin is easily the most recognized star of the silent era. The character he created—The Little Tramp—has been loved by generations and no doubt will be discovered and loved by generations to come. Charlie Chaplin's films are timeless and need no historical context or scene setting to help us simultaneously find them funny and touching. But, it is useful to know Chaplin's background.

Chaplin came from a genteel but poor family. His parents were entertainers in the English music halls of the 1890s. His father was an alcoholic and left Charlie's mother when Charlie was just a few years old. When she wasn't in a hospital or committed to an institution, she taught Charlie and his brother how to sing and dance.

At times Chaplin lived with his mother, at others with his father or in orphanages. From time to time, he lived on the streets, sleeping in doorways and the parks of London and often going hungry. His childhood colored his view of the world and you can see it in his films. The villains are often petty, uncaring bureaucrats. Always, the uncaring are the villains.

In many of Chaplin's films, the tramp is terribly hungry. In *The Gold Rush*, he is so hungry, he becomes delusional, fantasizing that his prospecting partner is a plump chicken. Among his many food fantasies in *Modern Times* is a dream where he can pluck oranges off a tree through a window of his home while his suburban wife fries up a steak.

The heroines of *The Circus* and *Modern Times* are continually hungry and abused until the tramp shows up and provides for them in his own special way. Hunger was something Charlie knew very well growing up. For him, hunger was basic. It was visual and could represent everything the tramp lacked.

If the tramp was hungry, obviously there was no one to take care of him. He had no home, no loved ones, no job, no friends, nothing. When the heroines of *The Circus* and *Modern Times* are hungry, it is also clear that they are unloved, uncared for and unappreciated. When the little tramp provides food for them, it shows his basic human concern and touches our hearts.

Because of his mother's training, Chaplin was able to begin working as a stage performer at an early age. In his teens, he was the star of one of the leading music hall troupes in England. In America, the English music hall style of entertainment was known as vaudeville. In a way, vaudeville was similar to television—mass entertainment catering to the broadest popular tastes.

Vaudeville was a collection of short, fast-paced, live performances, each lasting roughly 10 minutes. One act might be a magician, then a singer, followed by a juggler and an animal act and so on, all in rapid fire. Admission was relatively cheap, about the price of the movies. However, the movies would eventually push vaudeville into oblivion.

Physical comedians and comedy were staples of vaudeville and English music halls. The falls, fights and tumbling—aptly called knock-about comedy—required tremendous acrobatic skills as well as a comedian's sense of timing. It is easy to see why this type of training spawned two of the great silent comics—Chaplin and Keaton.

In 1913, Mack Sennett, the creator of the Keystone Cops, saw Chaplin during an American tour and invited him to Hollywood to make films. Chaplin would never return to the stage. He had found his medium and the world loved the little tramp he created in his second film. By 1915, he would be an international star.

Chaplin's salary was $250 a month his first year at Keystone. Three years later, he would sign with Mutual for $55,000 a month. At the time, a round trip, first class ticket on an ocean liner to England cost $250. The little tramp was the highest-paid entertainer in the world.

For the next 25 years, Chaplin would be synonymous with comedy. When Chaplin started making movies, they were very different than they are today. Most films were one-reelers, 10 to 12 minutes long. Feature length films were mostly filmed version of plays. By 1913, the movies had found a commercial niche, but the glamour of Hollywood was in the future. Chaplin had no idea what his quick fling with movies would mean.

Chaplin wrote and starred in more than 35 one-reelers during his first year with Sennett. This was the pace of one-reelers. You would literally dream up a story line and gags on Monday and Tuesday, shoot on Wednesday, edit on Thursday and have your film in the theaters the following week.

Silent comedy lent itself to one-reelers. The story lines were mainly vehicles on which to hang the gags. Chaplin said that all he needed to make a film was a girl, a park and a cop . . . and of course the tramp.

Chaplin's success allowed him to become independent. By 1920, he was completely in control of his films, producing and distributing now as well as acting, directing, and writing. He was a complete one man movie company.

Now he could make films when and how he wanted. Chaplin was the first silent comedian to make feature-length comedy films. He made just a few films in the '20s and three films in the '30s, but there is not a turkey in the bunch. For 20 years, Chaplin would make nothing but critical and box office successes that have remained timeless masterpieces.

The coming of sound in 1927 did not stop Chaplin from making the kinds of films he loved. *City Lights*, *The Great Dictator* and *Modern Times*, made long after the coming of sound, are simply great films. But times change and the few films Chaplin made after 1940 do not meet the standards of his earlier work.

Chaplin started making films before Buster Keaton and Harold Lloyd, two other silent comic geniuses, and would keep making great films after Keaton and Lloyd had been stopped by the coming of sound.

BUSTER KEATON

Like Chaplin, Buster Keaton grew up in vaudeville. He was part of the family act by the time he was three. By reputation, it was one of the roughest acts in vaudeville. Buster was literally flung about the stage by his parents. By his teens, Buster Keaton was a skilled physical comedian with a well-developed comic persona. He was known as the great stone face since his character never acknowledged the disasters that happened around him.

Keaton started making films a few years after Chaplin and never went back to vaudeville. His films generally take place on a larger canvas than Chaplin's. Props for Keaton could easily involve speeding trains, a collapsing building or a cast of thousands.

HAROLD LLOYD

The third major silent comedian of the 1920s, Harold Lloyd, started not in vaudeville but in film as something of a Chaplin clone. Once he developed his own screen character with horn-rimmed glasses, he equaled Chaplin at the box office. The glasses gave Lloyd a vulnerability to go with his upbeat enthusiasm. Unlike Chaplin, Lloyd thinks that he can win the big game, the big house, and the pretty girl, if only he tries hard enough.

His character is not poor, downtrodden or hungry like the little tramp, but simply wants a bigger, better future. His character caught America's mood during the go-go, roaring '20s.

One of the most enduring images we have from silent comedies is Harold Lloyd hanging high above the city, clinging to the hands of a clock.

Though Keaton and Lloyd would continue to make films after the coming of sound, their best work was behind them.

CITY LIGHTS

City Lights was Chaplin's first movie after the coming of sound, but it was made in the silent style. The opening scene with the dedication of a statue by city officials would be Charlie's comment on the idea that movies should talk. For Chaplin, dialogue was unnecessary. To understand the officials, it is not necessary to hear their words, but only the shrill sound of a kazoo that doubles as dialogue. Comically, Chaplin has told us all that we need to know. It is funny and penetratingly truthful. Even after the coming of sound, the little tramp never speaks. In *Modern Times,* made after *City Lights*, the little tramp does sing a song with nonsense words and pantomime that shows how superfluous words really are.

One of the underlying themes in *City Lights* is that society is blind to the virtues and worth of someone who looks like the tramp. The rich man is only generous when he is blind drunk. The blind girl thinks Chaplin is rich and handsome. One of the powers of this film is the ending. Now that the girl can see, will she really be able to see the tramp for who he is? And what then?

The boxing match sequence in particular is a good example of Chaplin's comic genius and physical dexterity. We can see why W. C. Fields admiringly called Chaplin a blankity-blank ballet dancer.

The way Charlie worked was to become enthusiastic about a comic idea and then develop it. He filmed as he developed the story line and comedy gags, elaborating and refining as long as it took. The boxing match sequence took weeks to complete.

One simple shot at the end of *City Lights*, where the blind girl gives the Tramp a flower and then slowly realizes who he is, was redone for days until it was right. The shot, though simple, was absolutely crucial to making the whole film work. It needed to be perfect and Chaplin knew it. He was patient and stubborn enough to shoot film and spend his own money until it was perfect.

FEATURE FILMS

Chaplin and the other silent comedians did not start making feature-length films until the form had been well established. Developing the narrative structure for a 90-minute comedy is much tougher than for a dramatic story. Comedy is still the toughest art form today.

Most of the silent films from this era and their stars have long been forgotten. Chaplin, however, as the little tramp, has endured and touches us as effortlessly as he first did so long ago.

THE SILENT FRAME

Surprisingly, there are differences in the ways that silent comedies and sound comedies are shot. When sound replaced the silent cinema, the very framing and rhythms of film changed. Because silent comedy was funny visually, the punch line to the joke was often not centered on the character but involved the whole frame with everything very carefully arranged. Generally, to be funny, silent comedy used a wider frame than sound comedy.

For instance, in *The General* by Buster Keaton, one of the best jokes involves Keaton, a cannon and two speeding locomotives, one chasing the other. For the joke to work, it is necessary to have both trains in the frame at the same time. It is a very rare sound film that necessitates the scale of two speeding trains to tell a joke.

Buster Keaton being chased by one cop is not particularly funny. But in *Cops*, it is funny when Keaton is chased by scads of cops stretching for blocks across a wide city boulevard. It is funny visually. Johnny Depp being chased by scads of natives in *Pirates of the Caribbean, Dead Man's Chest* is an example of the kind of visual humor that was common in the silent era but basically disappeared with the coming of sound. It is not by accident that Johnny Depp runs in an exaggerated manner reminiscent of the silent era. Silent comedians knew what was funny.

All the great silent comics used a wide frame at times to be funny. In *The Kid*, Chaplin raced across roof tops to catch up with a truck to rescue his adopted son. We see Chaplin running and clambering across the rooftop and see the truck simultaneously. It is funny, touching, and suspenseful at the same time. In *Modern Times*, when Chaplin is roller skating blindfolded next to a chasm, it is crucial that we see Chaplin and the chasm simultaneously. Because he is moving so quickly on the skates, the frame needs to be quite wide for the humor to work. In the boxing sequence in *City Lights*, the humor comes not from the two opponents punching each other but from the dance between the two boxers and the referee. The humor is all visual.

In many of Harold Lloyd's best films, we need to see the physical jeopardy for the humor to work. In the famous scene where he is hanging from the hands of the clock, it is crucial that we see the ground so very far below him to make the scene funny. Of course, not all comedies in silent films required a wide frame. But the crucial point is that few sound films require a wide frame to be funny.

Sound films work differently. The humor is verbal, generally, and we often need to see both the speaker and who they are talking with simultaneously. That is, we need to see the delivery as well as the reaction to get the humor. The punch line is verbal and we want to see how the characters respond. So with the arrival of the sound era, the medium shot became more and more dominant. Over the years, sound film has developed a language that is substantially different from silent film. Year by year, the framing has become tighter and tighter, closer and closer. There is more visual impact as the camera comes closer. Today there is a great deal of visual punch in the way films are shot. They are closer, with more camera movement, and pack more visual punch. But what was lost is how to tell a joke visually.

Today wide shots are mostly just mundane framings to let you know where the characters are, to give you a sense of place, to establish a location. At times, wide shots may be used to give a sense of majesty or epic grandeur, such as in the battle scenes in *Lord of the Rings*. But it is a rare, rare film today that understands that framing can be funny. There are visual jokes and puns to be had. The silent comedy understood this in ways that have been forgotten.

The other framing necessary for silent film was the close-up. Now, of course, all films use close-ups almost from the beginning as significant visual punctuation. Close-ups are literally what allow the audience to feel close to characters, to understand them, and to get to know them better. In silent comedy, the visual jokes are usually wide but the character development comes through close-ups. Mellow dramas with their emotional emphasis also tended to rely on close ups to punctuate their stories.

TRIVIA

Virginia Cherrill, the star of *City Lights*, was one of the few leading ladies in whom Chaplin did not have a romantic interest. In fact, they did not get along very well. Charlie had met her at a party and invited her for a screen test.

Virginia was not that interested in being an actress and did not care about becoming a star. She came from a wealthy Chicago family and did not have to work for living, but she was one of the few actresses whom Charlie tested who could convey naturally and without affectation the idea that she was blind.

Several weeks into the shooting, Chaplin fired her. She simply did not work as hard as Chaplin wanted. He tested other actors but decided that Virginia was best and rehired her.

City Lights was the first film Chaplin made during the sound era. He did not care, and released the film to large box office success when the rest of Hollywood had converted to sound.

C H A P T E R 4
THE SILENT ERA

The Crowd

The time from *The Birth of a Nation* to the end of the silent era was incredibly brief, just 13 years. In that short span of time, film leapt from an uncertain future to a sophisticated visual medium that captivated audiences around the world. By 1927, Hollywood had gone from obscure California suburb to the glamour capital of the world. Comedies, westerns, science fiction, action, fantasies, dramas— it did not matter. Filmmakers around the world knew how to communicate with silent, moving pictures.

THE CROWD

1927 would be the last year of the silent era and its peak as an art form. One of the best from this last year is *The Crowd*. Even for audiences today, *The Crowd* is engaging and watchable. It is cinematic storytelling at its best. *The Crowd* blends a touching human story with powerful yet subtle visual details, special effects and a moving, vital camera without the overly-dramatic mannerism of some silent cinema. Yet it is a silent film from conception to execution.

The story, though common enough in everyday life, is rarely told in the movies. In the film boy meets girl, boy gets girl, and then they go about the business of trying to build a meaningful life together. With an exception or two nothing dramatic happens. There are no major vices, no affairs, no murders. A loving couple simply tries to get ahead in the go-go years of the roaring '20s. The film asks a simple question: is material success necessary for personal happiness? What about all the people who have the dream and the ambition but not the ability or luck to succeed? They can be smart, talented and charming—a loving father and husband but somehow unable to click in the rat race of corporate success.

The Crowd is a visual in ways that would be lost with the coming of sound. The geometric layout of the scenes in the maternity room, corporate offices and the couple's meeting outside the downtown skyscraper tells the story without saying a word. These kinds of visual elements disappear in the early sound films as the preoccupation with dialogue and the needs of the microphone overpower the images. It would be years before movies recaptured this kind of visual power.

A DIFFERENT ART FORM

Silent films were not just movies without sound. First, silent film was not silent. Usually there was live music to go along with the film. For major big-budget productions a large orchestra often would play along with the film. By the 1920s, more than 20,000 musicians, mostly piano players, had fulltime jobs playing in film theaters around the country. Sometimes actors would provide dialogue for the film, performing behind the screen, adding another dimension to the experience. There often were special sound effects, created live and in sync with the film as it played. At the very least, records were played along with the film. Silent film was anything but silent.

THE COMING OF SOUND

Even though the phonograph was invented a decade and a half before the first moving pictures, it would be another 50 years before reliable, synchronous sound would make it to the movies. There were a number of significant and formidable technological hurdles that had to be overcome before sound came to film. Systems had to be invented that could record, edit and distribute pictures and sound in perfect synchronization. The change, when it came, would be rapid and radical.

From the beginning, Edison had tried to produce synchronous sound. It was so tangibly close. There was the phonograph and the ability to record and play back sound. There was the ability to record and play back moving images. What was lacking was the ability to reliably put the two together. It took much longer and was much more difficult to combine sound and picture than it was to develop either of the parent technologies.

When film first began, cameras and projectors were hand cranked. Hand cranking was cheap, light and reliable. In 1900 electricity was still relatively rare and unreliable. Most cities were still converting from gas to electricity for lighting. Plus, in the early years, there were no small, dependable electric motors for the projectors and cameras. It was difficult enough to guarantee an electric light source to project a moving image to an audience. Most theaters had bulky, nasty chemical batteries as backup in these beginning years. In 1900 electrification of cities was a dream; by 1920 it was the norm. Electricity and the movies developed simultaneously and for good reason.

Slight visual variations in frame rates produced by hand cranking during recording and play back went unnoticed by an audience. But sound requires absolute consistency between playback and recording speeds. Slight fluctuations in speed will immediately be heard. The sound becomes higher if the speed increases, and lower if the sound slows down, even if it is just a bit. Sound requires rock-steady consistent speeds from original recording to final projection. Hand cranking with the obvious potential for human inaccuracy simply will not work.

In 1900, even though telephones carried and amplified sound electrically, the transmission had to be continually boosted to cover any distance. To adapt this infant technology so that it was capable of producing reasonable quality sound for theater audiences took a while. In fact, it took quite a while. Ultimately what it took was the invention of the vacuum tube and the skyrocketing demand for radio.

Starting in 1915, radio quickly became a huge consumer product. Radios escalating the demand for speakers and clear, amplified sound provided the economic incentives that led directly to high quality sound for the movies.

MOVING PICTURES

In an interesting contradiction, movies are really a series of still photographs that, when played back, give the appearance of fluid movement. This is an artifact of human physiology. The process of making images move, then, is a process of starting and stopping. A frame of film is fed to a precise location behind the lens where it is held for a fraction of a second while a shutter opens, exposing the film to light. The shutter closes and a new frame is fed into place, and so on. In silent film, the frame rate was roughly 16 frames per second. In sound films the rate is 24 still frames per second.

Sound is exactly the opposite. It must be recorded continuously with no starting or stopping. So the difficulty was in recording sound and pictures on two separate systems that could be rejoined and kept in sync. And it does not take much to be out of sync. Just one frame off and the result is "lip flap." Not only is "lip flap" annoying but it ruins the effect, making any film silly and laughable. It was a formidable task to keep 100 minutes of film or nearly 140,000 frames in exact sync.

Perhaps for modern audiences it is difficult to remember a time before audio tape and digital recording. But even audio tape is a relatively recent innovation. The sounds for the films of the 1930s were recorded on cumbersome wax or lacquer records, discs and cylinders with vibrating needles capturing and reproducing the sound.

AUDIENCES

During the 1920s, box office returns went up every year. Every year Hollywood sold more tickets and made more money. There was no demand for sound until one film caught the world's attention. Synchronous sound for film had been around as a novelty in various forms before *The Jazz Singer* changed forever how films are made. *The Jazz Singer* basically was a silent film with some sound elements, mostly singing and a few words of dialogue. But it was enough. After *The Jazz Singer*, sound became mandatory.

Many in the industry thought sound would be just a passing novelty; many hoped it would be. But audiences quickly decided that, given the choice between silent film and talkies, they preferred sound. Audiences may not demand innovations but they know what they like. And they liked sound. Box office returns quickly confirmed that sound was the future and the silent film era was over.

SOUND

Sound changed Hollywood forever and in many unexpected ways. Whole new genres would spring up almost immediately, while other kinds of stories would slowly fade away. For a while, at least, dialogue would be more important than the visuals. The coming of sound also would make films more national. Silent film language was universal, so in the silent era there was no foreign film. Country of origin did not matter. Silent acting and storytelling was universal. Title cards, of course, needed to be translated from country to country. But title cards are cheap to change. A star like Charlie Chaplin could be seen and loved everywhere without regard to language or culture.

Sound would change all that, making it particularly difficult for foreign films to be successful in America. Interestingly enough, the coming of sound did not hurt Hollywood in foreign markets. After the coming of sound, much would change in Hollywood. What would not change is that Hollywood would continue to dominate movies around the world.

TRIVIA

MGM only made *The Crowd* because King Vidor, one of its top directors, insisted. Even so, MGM changed the ending many times to make it more marketable.

Many of the scenes in New York were shot with a hidden camera to show real crowds on real streets with real traffic—highly unusual for the time.

In 1927, *The Crowd* and *Sunset* each won an Academy Award for a category that no longer exists—Artistic Quality of Production. That same year *Wings* won for Best Picture—the only year a film without dialogue would win a Best Picture Award.

Surprisingly, as part of the director's quest for realism, this is the first American film to show a toilet.

CHAPTER 5

THE COMING OF SOUND

Scarface

Courtesy of the John Springer Collection/Corbis.

The coming of sound was more than just a stunning technological advance. Sound was not just a dramatic achievement that made the movies more lifelike, but almost immediately new genres and stories hit the screens and thrilled audiences. Some like the musical are obvious. It's hard to imagine a silent musical, but others like the gangster film and romantic comedy are subtler and provide insights into the significant difference between silent film and talkies. The coming of sound did nothing less than revolutionize Hollywood. Sound, dialogue, banter, verbal jokes, word play, accents, slang, verbal intonation and much, much more were not just added to the visuals, but reinvented film.

THE LOSS

One way to understand the difference between sound film and silent film is to see what was lost. Immediately, of course, sound caused language problems that did not exist in the silent era. Film was no longer a world art form but became very narrowly national. There were other slower, subtler changes. Over the next decade the great silent comedians would fade from the screen and not be replaced. Physical humor will always be a part of film comedy, but with sound verbal humor was emphasized and physical humor seemed passé, slightly crude and used more as visual punctuation. Audiences still love the falls and spills but sound films would need a lot more than just a series of clever stunts to be successful at the box office.

With the coming of sound, melodrama, like physical comedy, slowly faded from Hollywood film over the next few decades. Melodrama was uniquely suited to the silent era. After all, emotional trauma and drama could and was played out on the faces of the actors. No words were necessary to convey deep, traumatic emotional loss. Heartbreaking drama and melodrama, like physical comedy, did not disappear completely but slowly became supporting elements in film and lost the dominance they had during the silent years.

During the 1920s, women were the box office equals of men. Leading actresses were as popular and made as much money as the men. Slowly over the next two decades women's roles in film became more and more subservient to men's roles. Slowly, they lost box office clout, made less money than men and saw their onscreen roles fade away. The silent film was well-suited to telling women's stories. Partly because women's lives were so often wrapped in emotion that could be shown in the faces of the actors, the silent era produced many star vehicles for women. The change was not sudden, but by the 1950s women would not be the financial box office stars that they were during the 1920s. There were always important women stars, but after the 1920s, the breadth of roles and the number of top female box office performers slowly shrank decade by decade.

Visually it would take a decade or so for film to regain the power that it had in the silent era. The needs of the microphone and a sound-proof recording area for noisy cameras limited the freedom of movement that came so easily to the small hand-cranked cameras of the silent era. Sound cameras were big, bulky, heavy and for some years had to be in their own sound-proof area separated from the shooting by a glass window. The first talkies were static and almost wall-to-wall dialogue. But with time and experience Hollywood learned how to use sound and then relearned how to move the camera.

THE GAIN

Gangster films were not successful in the silent era, yet quickly became huge hits with the coming of sound. It is easy to see why gangster films never caught on during the silent era. Too much is missing from a silent gangster film that we take for granted in films like *Scarface*. To make an effective gangster film you need the rat-a-tat-tat of machine guns, booming explosions, squealing tires, car crashes, plus the distinctive gangster patter. "You dirty rat" or "Take 'em for a ride" does not work on a title card. It needs to be delivered with a snarl and Bronx accent. Even "yeah" delivered by the right actor can be very effective dialogue.

SCARFACE

Scarface, one of the best of the early gangster films, was based loosely on the life of Al Capone with a little of the rumored sexual proclivities of the 16th century Italian Borgias thrown in for flavor. It was an effective combination—subliminal sexual desires and current events ripped from the headlines. Audiences in the 1930 were very familiar with Al Capone's career. It was no secret that he was the leading mobster in Chicago. It was also no secret how he got to be the leading mobster in Chicago. Everybody knew who he was and who he killed to get there. He was famous. Events in *Scarface,* like the Saint Valentine's Day massacre and other notorious murders, were in the newspaper headlines. Most people knew that Capone was behind these famous murders, though of course, in Hollywood fashion, the facts in *Scarface* were altered, expanded and distorted, not to protect the innocent, but to streamline and heighten the drama. Years after *Scarface* was made, Capone went to jail for income tax evasion.

Scarface is only one of a number of gangster films made in the early 1930s. They were very popular and provided the springboard to careers for a number of new Hollywood stars. Their success would ultimately lead to their demise. After the mid 1930s, with the coming of new self-imposed censorship guidelines, the gangster film of the early 1930s would abruptly disappear.

CENSORSHIP

Many people thought that films like *Scarface* glorified the gangsters and undermined the morals of the country. Even though the gangster usually died at the end, the moral tone of the films was disturbing. The men and women of the gangster film were ruthlessly selfish, greedy, violent, and promiscuous with no sense of loyalty or code of ethics. The whole tone of the gangster films reeked of an amoral, laissez faire attitude towards conscience, sex and violence. In the gangster films, violence and duplicity paid off big in fancy cars, beautiful homes, power, and sexy girlfriends. Gangsters had no conscience and no moral framework. They simply took what they wanted without regard for friendship or a code of honor.

One of the major problems in *Scarface* is that the hero of the film is a cold blooded killer who is able to thumb his nose at societal conventions, double cross and steal the girlfriend of his business partner, kill his best friend and lust after his own sister. The police seem powerless. No one seems to be a match for Tony Cumonte. There is no one on the right side of the law able to stop him. Ultimately he self destructs, but not because the police or the powers of the righteous are able to contain him. Not a comforting idea that criminals are more powerful than justice and society's only hope is that they make some fatal, stupid mistake.

In the western film there is a code of conduct that may or may not be ignored but it is recognized by outlaw, gunslinger and lawman alike. In the gangster film, there was no code, except kill or be killed and grab as much as possible. The gangster was not the western gunslinger in an urban setting. The gangster was a totally new, modern character without creed or code. Very disturbing.

During the great depression, when at times more than 20 percent of the population was unemployed, the ability to take and not worry about consequences or conscience was appealing and glamorous. Many in society thought these amoral gangster films were dangerous. Films like *Scarface* generated a great deal of criticism and helped motivate and organize the forces that pushed Hollywood within a few years to radically change the kinds of films it made.

CENSORSHIP AND THE COMING OF SOUND

As often happens, changes in technology had unexpected consequences. The coming of sound for the movies in 1927 led directly to the restrictive censorship codes of the mid-1930s.

The Hollywood studios were not eager to make sound films. But after *The Jazz Singer*, it was clear that sound was here to stay. All the studios embarked on crash programs to convert to sound. Silent films already in the can were reshot in sound.

Converting to sound was not cheap, easy or just a matter of adding a few microphones and recording devices. The stages where films were shot had to be soundproofed. All the lighting had to be replaced. The arc lights of the silent era gave off beautiful light but sputtered and hissed loudly. The new incandescent lights burned much hotter, producing lots more heat than the old arc lights, so the sound stages had to be air conditioned as well as soundproofed. Because all the studios owned numerous theaters, they also had to pay to convert the movie houses to sound.

Writers who could write dialogue had to be brought in from Broadway. In the silent era scripts were usually just story outlines that might run 10 or 20 pages. Now, with the addition of dialogue, scripts usually ran 90 to 100 pages and took much longer to write.

Even the cost of film stock went up, since silent film ran at 16 frames a second and sound film runs at 24 frames per second. More film was needed for both shooting and release prints, bumping the cost of film stock by more than 30%.

The studios borrowed heavily to convert to sound. Most had nearly completed the conversion by 1929 when the stock market crash sent the country into the Great Depression. For the studios, the Great Depression could not have come at a worse time. They had just borrowed huge amounts of capital and by the early '30s, box office receipts were declining.

To attract audiences, the studios became bolder and more daring in their stories. Sex and violence escalated on the screen. Films like *Scarface* were wildly popular but they also produced a significant moral backlash. Many were concerned that gangster films and others featuring promiscuous sex were undermining the morals of the country and were corrupting the nation's youth.

As sexual content and violence grew more blatant in the movies, there was a growing threat of boycotts by organizations such as the Catholic Legion of Decency. In the early '30s, Warner Brothers, the producers of *Scarface*, became ensnarled in a dispute with the Roman Catholic Bishop of Philadelphia. The bishop made attending a Warner Brothers film a mortal sin. Box office receipts dropped 50 percent in Pennsylvania.

This was very similar to the kind of public pressure that the Moral Majority in the 1990s was able to bring on 7-11 stores to get them to remove "Playboy" and "Penthouse" from their magazine racks, or the controversy today over violence in video games and the lyrics in pop music. Just like the music and video game industries today, Hollywood in the '30s responded to public pressure and the threat of boycotts with self censorship.

THE PRODUCTION CODE

In the mid-'30s, all the studios signed a document saying that they would make movies within a specific set of guidelines called the Production Code. As you can see below, the Production Code was far-reaching and covered much more than just sex and violence.

Provisions of the Code

*The Production Code enumerated three "General Principles":

1. No picture shall be produced that will lower the moral standards of those who see it. Hence the sympathy of the audience should never be thrown to the side of crime, wrongdoing, evil or sin.
2. Correct standards of life, subject only to the requirements of drama and entertainment, shall be presented.
3. Law, natural or human, shall not be ridiculed, nor shall sympathy be created for its violation.

Specific restrictions were spelled out as "Particular Applications" of these principles:

· Nudity and suggestive dances were prohibited.
· The ridicule of religion was forbidden, and ministers of religion were not to be represented as comic characters or villains.

---

*Courtesy of Wikipedia

- The depiction of illegal drug use was forbidden, as well as the use of liquor, "when not required by the plot or for proper characterization."
- Methods of crime (e.g. safe-cracking, arson, smuggling) were not to be explicitly presented.
- References to "sex perversion" (such as homosexuality) and venereal disease were forbidden, as were depictions of childbirth.
- The language section banned various words and phrases that were considered to be offensive.
- Murder scenes had to be filmed in a way that would discourage imitations in real life, and brutal killings could not be shown in detail.
- The sanctity of marriage and the home had to be upheld.
- Adultery and illicit sex, although recognized as sometimes necessary to the plot, could not be explicit or justified and were not supposed to be presented as an attractive option.
- Portrayals of miscegenation were forbidden.
- "Scenes of Passion" were not to be introduced when not essential to the plot. "Excessive and lustful kissing" was to be avoided, along with any other treatment that might "stimulate the lower and baser element."
- The flag of the United States was to be treated respectfully, as were the people and history of other nations.
- "Vulgarity," in a classic oxymoron, had to be treated within "the dictates of good taste."

Not only were many activities banned, but a particular world view and morality was enforced. The censor not only prevented certain images and stories from being told but required particular outcomes and morality in all films for everyone. The censor became part of the assembly line process of the studio system. For the next 30 years, Hollywood would make films within a very narrow range and with very predictable stories and outcomes.

HOWARD HAWKS

Howard Hawks had the good fortune to be born relatively rich. That gave him the ability to be independent in a Hollywood that preferred to sign directors to long-term, exclusive contracts and then dictate the kinds of films they could make. Most Hollywood directors chafed and struggled inside the Hollywood studio system but usually to little avail. Financially independent, Howard Hawks never became a contract director forced to do what studio executives demanded. Unlike most directors of the time, he was always able to work on films that interested him.

Howard Hawks is also unusual in that he directed so many good films in such a wide variety of genres: *Scarface*—gangster film, *The Dawn Patrol* and *Sergeant York*—war films, *Bringing Up Baby* and *His Girl Friday*—screwball comedy, *The Big Sleep*—film noir, *Red River*—western, and *To Have and Have Not*—romantic adventure. All are some of the best of their kind ever made. Not only did his work escape the narrow focus forced on most directors, but his work spanned three decades. It is the rare director that year after year, decade after decade, makes films that audiences and critics enjoy and appreciate. It is even rarer when, decades later, audiences and critics still enjoy and appreciate their work.

TRIVIA

Scarface screenwriter Ben Hecht was a former Chicago journalist familiar with the city's Prohibition-era gangsters.

Several Chicago gangsters worked as "consultants" during the shooting.

The film was released without censor approval. The movie's subtitle, "The Shame of a Nation," was added to deflect criticism that the film glorified crime.

"X" was used in a number of scenes because newspapers at the time would mark an "X" on the photo at the spot where a body was found.

Al Capone was rumored to have liked the film so much that he had his own copy of it.

George Raft, who played the best friend, was mainly a dancer and bit player before this film gave him a life-long Hollywood career.

Supposedly, George Raft's character Guido's coin flipping in the film was based on the mannerism of a small-time gangster George knew growing up in Hell's Kitchen in New York.

There were also rumors that Howard Hawks gave George that coin flipping bit of business because he was not a very good actor.

CHAPTER 6

PRE-CODE FILMS

Red Dust and *Trouble in Paradise*

Courtesy of Bettman/Corbis.

Courtesy of Paramount/The Kobal Collection.

From roughly 1930 to 1935, Hollywood made films unlike any before or since. As a group, these films are called pre-code films because they were made before the imposition of the Production Code that established strict, inflexible standards of censorship for all Hollywood films. What makes these pre-code films unique is that at the time, nobody in Hollywood knew they were doing anything particularly special. It was just business as usual, Hollywood making films to sell tickets and please their audiences. Hollywood was not purposely trying to make controversial or disturbing films, they were just trying to make money. Audiences liked a little sex and violence in their films and Hollywood has always tried to make what audiences liked.

A significant number of well-organized religious groups strongly objected to the amoral tone of many of these films. Though numerically in the minority, the breadth and depth of the opposition was significant and nationwide. Finally, because of mounting pressures, Hollywood agreed to self censorship because self censorship was better than Congressionally-imposed censorship or, even worse, censorship that varied from state to state, county to county, city to city. Almost overnight, Hollywood drastically changed the fabric of the films that were made.

There is a sense of freedom and breeziness to these pre-code films that disappeared with the coming of the Production Code. The Production Code not only severely restricted how sex and violence could be shown, but also required that positive behavior be rewarded and evil punished. After 1935, Hollywood films have a self-conscious air about them since all stories are forced down very narrow paths. The world of the Production Code is a world the way many wished it could be—a world they wanted, not the world that existed. It is a fantasy world where good triumphs, evil is vanquished, sex happens after marriage and "'til death do you part" is the goal.

After 1935 the subliminal goal of every romantic couple in every film is marriage. Before 1935 couples came together because they wanted to. There was no thought of marriage or long-term commitment. The couple just liked each other. Attraction and chemistry were enough. There was no concern about society or tomorrow. Characters in pre-code films were not necessarily promiscuous, but when they found someone to their liking it was enough.

Red Dust and *Trouble in Paradise* are the kinds of films where the moral tone offended many. In each, men and women come together for as long as it lasts. Marriage is not part of the agenda. It is not rejected. It is just unimportant, unworthy even of consideration. What matters to the couples in these films is that they admire each other, enjoy each other and will be together for as long as it works. Perhaps it is "'til death do you part" but not necessarily. Nor is it important.

These pre-code films captured an early '30s mentality that vanished with the coming of the Production Code. By the time the Production Code disappeared from Hollywood it was the late 1960s and the world was a very different place. It is not that Hollywood made terrible films after 1935. Or that the Production Code made it impossible to make films that touched audiences' hearts and influenced their lives. But there is no doubt that pre-code films are different from what comes after.

Pre-code films are to be enjoyed for what they were, a brief way of interpreting life that came to an abrupt end. What makes these films unique is that they captured a way of looking at the world, of morality and values that many found appealing, but was impossible for others to tolerate.

RED DUST

In *Red Dust*, Clark Gable moves from one woman to another as easily as changing his shirt. That the second woman is married is not particularly important to him, nor to the woman. Passion and connection are much more important. The leading characters in *Red Dust* have an earthy, healthy, unencumbered attitude toward sex, unrestricted by inconvenient moral strictures. Marriage? Unimportant. Social convention? Equally unimportant. They make no apologies and ask for no forgiveness. For them, morality does not enter into the question. Relationships are based ultimately on pragmatic passions and attractions.

Ultimately the woman's marriage becomes a lie and Clark Gable goes back to the first woman. She is a better match. She is a lot more like him—strong, independent, pragmatic and at ease with herself. Both live by their own rules without regard to societal niceties. One of the troubles of the characters is that they are too likable. They are generous, loyal, funny and charming but with their own sense of sexual morality. They are not evil, selfish, or unlikable, but their sexual code is their own. The concerns of society are not an issue and are not even considered. In *Red Dust*, adultery and living together do not matter. Going about the business of living is what is important. Moral codes are irrelevant. Many found this kind of independent thinking and living disturbing and intolerable.

TROUBLE IN PARADISE

In some ways the plot and amoral tone of *Trouble in Paradise* is even more disturbing than in *Red Dust*. In *Trouble in Paradise*, two carefree, professional thieves find love and connection without even a thought or hint of marriage. They live together, plot together, play together and steal together. It is enough. Marriage is not even an afterthought.

The thieving couple is attracted to each other in large part because they share a passion for stealing. It is their common bond. What's worse, they are attractive, charming, smart, witty and appealing. They are not evil, sociopaths, greedy or violent. They just prefer stealing to working.

As the story progresses, the leading man contemplates a romantic liaison with another woman, a rich young widow, not just for her money but because of their mutual attraction. What is even worse is that this smart, high-society woman is quite willing to have a romantic liaison simply because she wants to. There is no moral dilemma for her. No question, no second thought of why she should not spend the night together with her prospective lover. Why not? There is no good reason. Maybe it will work out, maybe not, but the sex comes first, then maybe a relationship. Perhaps there will be marriage; who knows and who cares?

This is a woman who should exemplify society's highest moral standards. Instead she sees nothing wrong in sex with someone she thinks is emotionally and physically attractive. Connection, chemistry, romance of course. Marriage why? It is not important that he is poor. It is not important that there will be marriage and finally it is unimportant that he is a thief. All this is very disturbing and ultimately unacceptable.

Neither of these films has any on-screen nudity or graphic violence, but their amoral tone was quite unsettling to many. They wanted moral virtue to triumph and sex out of marriage prohibited. Films with this kind of lackadaisical moral ethics were seen as undermining the moral health of the nation and were not to be tolerated.

There were many pre-code films that treated sex as light, uncomplicated, romantic connections with no real moral significance. They simply could not be made or even re-released after 1935. The Production Code did not prevent Hollywood from making great, popular films in the coming decades. Fantasy has always been what Hollywood was selling and there was no reality to the worlds of *Red Dust* and *Trouble in Paradise*. But what changed was the tone and the story arcs. Film for the next 30 years in Hollywood would be focused through the tight unyielding lens of the Production Code.

It was out of this kind of mindset that the romantic comedy of the 1930s, sometimes called screwball comedy, was born. The new romantic comedies gave up sex for words, fast pace and a new way of looking at social order.

ERNST LUBITSCH

Ernst Lubitsch, the director of *Trouble in Paradise*, was one of Hollywood's best during the 1930s. He was famous for his light, comedic touch. As a young man, he was a comic actor doing Jewish versions of Amos and Andy in Germany before switching to directing. He came to Hollywood in the early twenties already acknowledged as one of Germany's finest directors. He had a long and illustrious career in Hollywood and was head of production at Paramount for many years. In a famous quote that says as much about Hollywood as it does about Lubitsch, he is credited with saying "I've been to Paris France and I've been to Paris Paramount. Paris Paramount is better."

TRIVIA

Red Dust

When *Red Dust* was remade in 1953 as *Mogambo* and also starred Clark Gable, the Production Code forced significant changes to the story.

Red Dust is based on a play that opened in New York in 1928.

When the script underwent drastic re-writes, the role originally scheduled for Greta Garbo was recast with Jean Harlow.

Trouble in Paradise

Trouble in Paradise was based on a play, "A Becsuletes Megtalalo" (The Honest Finder) that opened in Budapest in 1931.

The movie could not be re-released after the imposition of the Production Code in 1935.

This film was selected to the National Film Registry, Library of Congress, in 1991.

CHAPTER 7
SCREWBALL COMEDY

It Happened One Night

Courtesy of Underwood and Underwood/Corbis.

It Happened One Night is one of those magical films that comes out of nowhere and changes Hollywood fundamentally and forever. It is hard to believe that it took a long time for Hollywood to make romantic comedies. Westerns had been around from the beginning. Epics, love stories, even horror films and sci-fi were well developed genres before the advent of the kind of romantic comedies that audiences ever since the 1930s have loved over and over.

The first film that put it all together was *It Happened One Night*. Made by poverty row studio Columbia Pictures, written and directed by Frank Capra, until then a small time director, the film won Academy Awards for best picture, best director, best actor and best actress. The film was a huge hit, much to the surprise of everyone connected with it.

Of course, there was always romance in most Hollywood films and they made lots of comedies. And certainly the two were often combined. But the specific kind of romantic comedy that became known as Screwball comedy started with one film, *It Happened One Night*.

Screwball comedy sounds like the films of the Marx brothers, The Three Stooges and Abbott and Costello, but actually screwball comedy is a form of romantic comedy that grew out of a number of trends in the 1930s.

Starting in the early 1930s, a number of factors including the Great Depression, new tight censorship codes, Hollywood's growing comfort with dialogue, and the legacy of the physical comedy of the silent era were combined to produce a new genre—screwball comedy. This is the genius of *It Happened One Night*. This film provided the blueprint for how to make romantic comedies in an era that had in essence outlawed sex outside of marriage.

CHARM OF SCREWBALL COMEDY

Love at first sight had been the cliché of film romances from early on. In film after film it was common for couples to be immediately attracted to each other and let their passions rule. First the couple comes together, then fate intervenes forcing them apart. The idea was the greater their ardor, the greater their suffering because they are apart.

There is no doubt these couples love each other. There can be misunderstandings and obstructing circumstances, but there is no doubt they want each other. Everything from *Cinderella* to *Romeo and Juliet* follows this basic story line.

Screwball comedy turned convention inside out. Generally at the beginning of most romantic comedies, the couple can not stand each other. It is only over time that they grow to understand, appreciate and then love each other. Why at least one half of the potential romantic couple wants nothing to do with the other is relatively unimportant. Sometimes it is class differences, sometime it is because the couples are married to each other and on the point of divorce, sometimes it is over silly misunderstandings. The why is unimportant. The intriguing discovery of screwball comedy was that you could make compelling romances out of couples who wanted no part of each other.

From a censorship point of view this made life very simple. It was easy to keep couples out of bed together when they did not like each other. Divorcing couples were a favorite because their separation allowed for all sorts of interesting situations and variations. Since they were married they could not become sexually involved with anyone else, though they could date. And there was always the potential of the divorcing couple reaffirming their love and getting back into bed together which was okay since they were married.

So, interestingly, a key ingredient that helped shape screwball comedy was the newly-adopted censorship guidelines—the Production Code. Because premarital sex and stories that reflected loose morals were no longer allowed after 1935, the verbal banter of the screwball comedies replaced sex. Instead of couples moving quickly to romantic involvement they were forced by circumstances to show their attraction through verbal sparring.

Since the Production Code required marriage before sex, if Hollywood wanted to add a little sexual intrigue to their films, couples had to be married. Divorcing couples allowed Hollywood to combine virtue, spice, temptations and finally sex in new and unique ways. Surprisingly this formula, first laid out so clearly in *It Happened One Night*, worked over and over again decade after decade.

CLASS AND SCREWBALL COMEDY

Another element in *It Happened One Night* that was used repeatedly was the antagonism that was produced by class differences. Often in screwball comedy what keeps the potential lovers apart is that they are from different classes—one poor, one privileged. It takes awhile for them to overcome the class differences.

One of the reasons screwball comedy in the 1930s was so popular was that it portrayed the rich as ditzy and out of touch with life. During the Great Depression, screwball comedy gave audiences a chance to laugh at the foibles of the rich and see that being rich meant losing touch with the world. Living in a mansion and having servants separated the wealthy from the world. It took someone with common sense to show the rich what they were missing.

During the Great Depression, audiences had no desire to see the rich as greedy, unfeeling and avaricious. A Marxist view of the wealthy as exploiters of the proletariat is not what the working class wanted to see. They wanted to see that their lives and values were worth more than mere money and wealth.

MARRIAGE AND COMEDY

If the pre-code films were unconcerned about marriage and societal conventions, Production Code films were obsessed with marriage. Almost every screwball comedy of the 1930s was, in one way or another, dealing with couples about to be married, about to be divorced, divorced and maybe remarrying, annulments and elopements. Of course every screwball comedy ends with the sanctity of marriage preserved.

DIALOGUE 1930s

By the mid-1930s, sound recording equipment and techniques had improved to the point that directors were able to make the movies move again. And they had become adept at blending visual gags typical of silent film with witty dialogue.

Now, almost 10 years after the coming of sound, writers had become good at writing fast-paced dialogue that suited the movies, instead of trying to mimic a Broadway theatrical production. Many of the early sound films were based on plays; now more and more films would be written just for the screen.

The dialogue of *It Happened One Night* snaps and crackles. Audiences of the '30s were accustomed to listening to radio in ways that audiences today do not. Much of the radio programming of the 1930s was verbal, either dramatic or comedy shows that audiences listened to with undivided attention. Today audiences are often multitasking, listening intermittently. The television, radio or computer is just providing background entertainment. The audience of the screwball comedy of the 1930s and 1940s appreciated the dialogue as much as the stars, the falls and the visuals.

FRANK CAPRA

Before *It Happened One Night*, the director Frank Capra was a relatively unimportant silent gag writer, most known for putting Laurel and Hardy together as a comedy team. For the rest of the 1930s he would be one of the most noted directors in Hollywood, turning out comedy after comedy that hit a nerve with audiences during the Great Depression. His phenomenal success at the box office almost single-handedly propelled Columbia into the front ranks of Hollywood studios.

TRIVIA

Clark Gable didn't want to do *It Happened One Night* and was sent to Columbia by MGM as punishment for complaining about the kind of films he was forced to make at MGM.

Gable didn't want to do *Gone with the Wind* either. He thought that was a woman's picture.

To give you an idea of how popular the film was, in one scene, Clark Gable takes off his shirt and he is not wearing an undershirt. According to Hollywood legend, the next year undershirt sales fell more than 25 percent. This kind of success guaranteed almost instant mimicry in Hollywood.

Director Frank Capra came up with the idea about "the walls of Jericho" because Claudette Colbert refused to undress in front of the camera.

There is a Nazi and a Bollywood version of *It Happened One Night* in addition to many other loosely-adapted versions.

CHAPTER 8

WESTERNS

Stagecoach

Courtesy of the John Springer Collection/Corbis.

The western is the granddaddy of all American genres. Almost from the beginning America cranked out westerns. By some estimates, 25 percent of all American films between 1900 and 1970s are westerns. No other genre has had this kind of longevity. Screwball comedy lasted 10 years, film noir, 10 years, and the musical, 30 years. Gangster pictures came in and out of fashion, but the western endured.

The same plots were done over and over: cattle ranchers vs. sheep herders, cowboy vs. Indians, and outlaws vs. the law. The variations and mutations were endless and popular. Besides all the Hollywood westerns, during the '50s and '60s there were scads of Westerns on television. Every night, and on every channel, there were westerns—"Gun Smoke," "Wagon Train," "Wanted: Dead or Alive," "Maverick," "Paladin" and many, many more. Now there are none. The Western, with a few exceptions, has disappeared.

Westerns no longer speak to us, yet their values and archetypes echo through current films. Most cop and detective films are just urban cowboy flicks. Films like *Star Wars* and *Star Trek* can easily be seen as space westerns.

END OF THE WESTERN

After surviving most of the 20th century, the Western finally succumbed and faded away. There were attempts at revivals with new twists, such as HBO's "Deadwood." They were the exceptions. Westerns died because they no longer offered the kinds of stories that matter to us. The situations are wrong, the outcomes are wrong and we have moved on.

The narrow stereotypes available for women in particular were too limiting. Women needed many more choices in character than prostitute/saloon girl or school teacher/gentle woman from the east. Even the roles for men were limited. Rancher or farmer, gun slinger or shop keeper, sheriff or outlaw, coward or hero. The roles and the situations no longer suited us.

The dangers in the western were clear and unambiguous. The difference between right and wrong was easy. There was no question as to what should be done. A fistfight or gun fight was all that was needed to set the world straight. Today moral choices are much more difficult. The scale of evil has grown exponentially and the response must equal the danger. Somehow, even the classic six-shooter seems almost like a toy, not to be taken seriously. Now we are worried about the threat of mega deaths.

Just as importantly we have come to see Native Americans in a very different light. They can no longer be the convenient, lawless savages. It is hard to look at Native Americans on the screen anymore without a twinge of nationalistic guilt and sadness at our collective historic behavior.

The Western will never go away completely. It is part of our history and Americans' images of themselves. But it's hard to foresee a future where westerns will have the impact on Hollywood and the country they had just a few decades ago.

THE ROOTS

At the turn of the century, dime novelists turned out scores of stories extolling the exploits of outlaws and lawmen like Billy the Kid, Jessie James and Wyatt Earp. From their imaginations came many of the motifs that we take for granted as part of the legend of the old west. The shootout on main street, quick-draw gun slingers and the western code of honor are all products of their fertile imagination.

STAGECOACH

Stagecoach is a classic western in this tradition with all the standard stuff. There are rampaging Indians, the cavalry riding to the rescue, a heroic outlaw, a lawman bending the rules, a saloon girl/prostitute with a heart of gold, and a proper lady.

The women in *Stagecoach* are typical western stereotypes. Dallas, the prostitute, grew up in the west. Besides sex, she knows that what a man in the west needs most is a gun and a horse. She gets both for John Wayne. To the Ringo Kid, her past as a saloon girl is unimportant. She is the kind of woman that a man in the west needs.

Mrs. Mallory, the woman of the east, is another stereotype and represents the coming of law and order, respectability and stifling moral codes. In most westerns, the woman of the east is a blond. The woman of the west usually has dark hair and is often part Indian or Mexican. Frequently, the saloon girl dies at the end of the film to make way for the woman of the east and the gunman rides off into the sunset alone.

This is the trade-off in most westerns. The coming of civility, schools and law means the loss of freedom and the imposition of traditional morality. Sex is for marriage and grudges are settled in court, not in the streets.

The birth of Little Coyote symbolizes the new generation born in the west. Son of a cavalry officer and an eastern gentle woman, nursed by a prostitute, delivered by an alcoholic doctor and born in the frontier, he is the ultimate western hybrid.

In *Stagecoach* and many westerns, the cavalry is the tool that tames the west. The cavalry suppresses the Indians so settlers can farm, raise cattle, build towns and establish law and order.

In a few westerns like *Little Big Man* and *Dances with Wolves*, the cavalry is a negative force, seen as an exterminating agent of US expansion.

In *Stagecoach*, the director, John Ford, takes these clichés and adds subtle nuances that are not part of most westerns. For instance, the scenes where everyone votes on the next course of action does many things. The characters explain their votes, deepening our understanding of them. It also adds to the underlying theme that everyone, sheriff, banker, saloon girl, gambler or gentle lady is equal in the wilderness.

Littered with stereotypes, what makes this film a masterpiece is the execution and subtle depth to the characters that John Ford brings to the film.

ROAD PICTURE

Stagecoach is really a number of genres blended together. Besides being a western, it is also a road picture. In a road picture, characters under duress travel from one location to the next and the ordeal transforms them. In *Stagecoach*, a number of characters find inner courage after their struggle in the wilderness. The whisky drummer, a milquetoast at the beginning, puts his foot down after the birth of Little Coyote. The alcoholic Doc Boone stands up to Luke Plummer and takes away his shotgun. The wilderness has brought out the heroic in each of them.

MISE-EN-SCENE

Mise-en-scene is a French term that simply means that everything in the frame, objects as well as the placement of actors, has meaning. In westerns, the landscape is often a crucial element of the mise-en-scene. In *Stagecoach*, the environment is majestic, stark and hostile. The soldiers and stagecoach are dwarfed by the magnificent buttes and mesas.

In wide shot after wide shot, Ford shows us just how insignificant human beings are in the vastness of the western wilderness. The cavalry and the stagecoach are mere specks in the arid wastelands of Monument Valley. To survive here, one must be tough, resilient and good with a gun.

JOHN WAYNE

Before *Stagecoach*, John Wayne was a nobody. Afterwards he was a star. For the next 30 years, he would be one of Hollywood's top box office performers. Decade after decade, in westerns or war pictures as a tough cop or just a tough guy, John Wayne was a star. Today he is remembered mostly for his westerns, but he played in all sorts of films.

Wayne got his start in the movies by accident. He was a football player at USC working as a grip on movie sets to make extra money during the summers. He was a big, likable, handsome guy with a good attitude, and worked for John Ford on a number of films. Over time, they developed a mutual fondness for each other that evolved into the affection between a father and son.

After Wayne got hurt and could no longer play football, Ford encouraged him to try his luck as an actor. Almost immediately, Wayne starred in a big budget silent western, *The Big Trail*. That film went nowhere and his career stalled for years in the twilight of one low-budget shoot-'em-up after another.

He even tried his hand at being a singing cowboy in the style of Roy Rogers and Gene Autrey. His name was Singing Sandy. After 10 years, Wayne was making a living as an actor, but was merely one of the faceless multitude that showed up in scads of low budget westerns. *Stagecoach* changed all that.

Stardom came late to Wayne, but once established, he quickly eclipsed the western heroes who came before him. As John Ford said, "it is hard to make a western without John Wayne."

JOHN FORD

John Ford was a top studio director for more than 40 years. He started in the silent era and made great films into the '60s. Today he is mostly remembered for his westerns. Certainly nobody made better westerns than Ford. *Stagecoach*, *My Darling Clementine*, *The Searchers* and *Who Shot Liberty Valance* are some of the best westerns ever made. But in his career, Ford made more than a hundred films, including excellent films such as *The Grapes of Wrath*, *How Green was My Valley* and *Young Mr. Lincoln*.

Ford is remembered for his subtle ability to develop characters and story elegantly with little dialogue. *Stagecoach* opens with a classic example of Ford's filmic economy. A telegraph operator listens to frantic clicks, looks alarmed, and says the wire has been cut. Then he says, "Only one word came through, Geronimo." That one word said it all.

Akira Kurosawa, the great Japanese director, was a huge fan and said that all of his films—but especially the samurai films—were influenced by Ford's work. Later, American directors like Francis Ford Coppola, Scorsese and Lucas said that Kurosawa's films were an inspiration for them.

George Lucas said that he took a Kurosawa samurai film called *Hidden Fortress* and adapted it into something called *Star Wars* where the swords become light sabers and two bumbling peasants become the robots C3PO and R 2 D 2.

Yojimbo, a samurai film by Kurosawa, was remade almost shot for shot as *A Fistful of Dollars* starring Clint Eastwood. It was shot in Spain with an Italian cast and director. Sixteenth century Japan became the American West. Swords became pistols, and a new western hero had been invented.

This is how film works. Great directors make great films that following directors see, admire and strive to emulate. This is not slavish imitation but inspiration. It is how the best elements of cinema move around the world, from generation to generation and from film to film.

TRIVIA

Stagecoach has been remade a number of times, once with Bing Crosby and Ann-Margret, and for television with Willie Nelson, Johnny Cash and Kris Kristofferson.

Neither retain the power of the original and the television version is at times laughable.

Hombre is a reasonably good take-off on the original where the Indians become bandits and Paul Newman, as a half-breed Indian agent, becomes the social outcast.

Stagecoach was based on a short story in Collier's called "Stage to Lordsburg," but a number of important changes were made.

Ford and his writer Dudley Nichols deleted two passengers, substituting the banker and the doctor for an Englishman and a cattleman. Also in the original short story, the eastern woman was not pregnant.

It is easy to see the effect these changes had. Doc Boone is a major character in the film and the pregnancy is an important plot device.

Ford originally wanted to do *Stagecoach* in color, but the studio did not want to spend that kind of money on a western with John Wayne, an unknown, as a leading actor.

Ford was unwilling to use someone else and made the picture in black and white as a compromise.

There is more to directing than just deciding where the camera goes.

Claire Trevor, John Carradine and Thomas Mitchell were some of Hollywood's best actors of the day. Wayne felt deeply inferior and his performance suffered.

So, though Ford was a mentor and a father figure to Wayne, he verbally abused Wayne unmercifully on the set. Ford called Wayne a lumbering lunkhead among many more vicious, vulgar names and continually rode him on the set.

Because of the harshness and unfairness of Ford's actions, the other actors became very protective of Wayne and went out of their way to help him in his role.

If Ford's true feelings were shown, it is likely that the other actors would have seen Wayne as the director's favorite. Instead, Ford got what he wanted from his actors and made a great western and a great film.

CHAPTER 9
HOLLYWOOD REBEL

Citizen Kane

Courtesy of Underwood and Underwood/Corbis.

Citizen Kane is probably the most influential film of the sound era, yet critics at the time were unimpressed. It was not a box office smash and it won one solitary Academy Award—for best screen play. Today, most critics consider *Citizen Kane* one of the greatest films ever made. Sixty years later it still inspires new film makers.

Few directors have ever tried to do what Orson Welles tried. As a brash 25-year-old, Welles thought he could change Hollywood film making. He did—just not the way he had intended. With the confidence of youth, Welles set out not only to make a great picture but to make one like no one else had ever done. And no one has come close to making a film like *Citizen Kane*.

INFLUENCES

For Welles and most of his cast, *Citizen Kane* would be their first film. All of Orson Welles' background in theater and radio show up in *Citizen Kane*. In scene after scene, the blocking of the characters is meticulously and carefully staged. Blocking is simply where the actors are positioned on the stage or in the shot.

In one famous shot, the camera starts on a young Kane playing outside in the snow with Rosebud, his sled. The camera slowly dollies back to frame the father, then the banker, then the mother, sitting at the dining room table. They are signing papers. The banker is between the mother and the father. Money has come between the family, leaving Kane out in the cold.

The soundtrack is rich, layered and textured, as befits someone with Welles' radio background. There are numerous telling audio cuts that condense time and yet are full with meaning—such as when Mr. Thatcher wishes Kane a Merry Christmas and the Happy New Year is many, many years later.

In Xanadu, Kane and Susan Alexander shout their conversations because they have grown so far apart.

The mise-en-scene is often telling. The sequence with Kane and his wife seated across from each other in front of the cavernous fireplace at Xanadu shows visually how far apart the couple is. The empty room mirrors how empty their lives have become.

Mrs. Kane's assembling jigsaw puzzles quickly and visually establishes not only how bored she is, but metaphorically resembles the audience's search to put the pieces of Kane's life into some meaningful order.

One of the most important influences of *Citizen Kane* was its look. The lighting is highly dramatic and similar to many of Welles' New York stage productions. This use of dark shadows and high contrast lighting is an influence from German expressionism of the 1920s. The Germans used lighting to convey mood and feeling and Welles loved it.

Greg Toland, the cinematographer of *Citizen Kane*, studied at Ufa, the major film studio in Germany. Toland, also young and brash, wanted to push Hollywood studio cinematography and lobbied to be assigned to Welles' production. He and Welles worked well together to establish the look of *Citizen Kane*. Welles often set the lights himself as he did for his stage productions and Toland would adjust them for film.

The moving camera and deep focus that are a hallmark of *Citizen Kane* had been done by Jean Renoir, in France, in the 1930s, but Welles and Toland pushed the limits, designing scene after scene with tremendous depth of focus.

It took will and desire to add this kind of depth to the frame. Toland used wide angle lenses, which provide for deeper focus but have a tendency to distort images. These lenses are used sparingly in feature films since they make the stars look less glamorous. But Welles did not care whether anyone was beautiful or handsome. He wanted the arrangement of the images to tell the story. And that's what he got.

They also increased the foot-candles of the lighting so they could shoot with higher f-stops to increase the depth of the focus, again going against normal studio practice.

Citizen Kane contains more than eight hundred processed special effects shots. Sometimes these are simple, like using split lenses or simple mattes, while others are more complicated setups using miniatures and animation. None of this is surprising from the studio that produced *King Kong*.

Welles' contract at RKO allowed him creative control as long as he stayed inside the budget, which at $860,000 was relatively modest considering what Welles was trying to do. He had an amazing amount of freedom for a 25-year-old first-time director.

Welles said that he watched John Ford's *Stagecoach* over and over to prepare himself for *Citizen Kane*. Like many filmmakers, he admired Ford's ability to develop depth for his characters quickly and elegantly.

What is apparent from viewing *Stagecoach* and *Citizen Kane* is the consistent use of low camera angles to make major characters seem large and powerful. Yet because of the ceilings in view just above their heads, they seem trapped and constrained by their environment.

This is how film imagery moves from one director to another, from one genre to another. Directors see something they like that produces an emotional response they want for their films, and they add it to their repertoire. This is the kind of impact *Citizen Kane* and Orson Welles had on the generations of filmmakers that followed.

FUTURE FILMMAKERS

Nobody has tried to make a film like *Citizen Kane* and it certainly stands alone as a biography. But film makers, for generations, have borrowed liberally from Welles' palette.

Film noir in particular owes much to *Citizen Kane* even though *Citizen Kane* is not film noir. Many of the important elements of *Citizen Kane* such as lighting, use of flashbacks, psychological motivation, and flawed heroes who fail all have become staples of film noir.

The writers and directors who created the noirs of the '40s did not know they were creating a new film style. They were simply reflecting the dark mood of a nation at war.

This was a war that saw millions of civilians killed, the methodical gassing and exterminating of whole populations in the Nazi death camps, and the dropping of atomic weapons on Japanese civilians.

Film noir is not as much a genre as a sensibility reflecting a pessimistic post-war mood. There are noir detective movies, noir westerns, even noir comedies.

Few films have the fractured structure of *Citizen Kane*, with its overlapping flashbacks, but many of the film noirs of the '40s begin with a character's death and then go back and trace the events that bring him to a tragic end.

At the beginning of *Sunset Boulevard*, the camera is at the bottom of a swimming pool, looking up at a fully clothed William Holden floating face-down. He is dead. In voice-over narration he says, "Bet you would like to know how I ended up here with three bullets in my back." The rest of the film tells his story.

In *DOA*, Edmond O'Brian walks into a police station and says he wants to report a murder. When the Police Sergeant asks whose, he says "Mine" and then relates the story of how he was poisoned. The film finishes with his death.

This sense of fatalism in noir like *Citizen Kane* comes from the flashbacks. At the beginning of the film, the character's fate is sealed. No heroism, nothing, can change their fate. All the audience can hope for is to learn what went wrong.

The lighting in film noir, like *Citizen Kane*, is often dramatic and high-contrast. These are black stories with a dark look.

It is hard to call them "heroes," but the protagonists of film noir are often like Charles Foster Kane; they are psychologically damaged. Unable to transcend their past, they fail.

CONTROVERSY

The back story of the making of *Citizen Kane* is shrouded in conflicting claims and controversy about who wrote what. Herman Mankiewicz and Welles shared writing credits and the Academy Award, but no one is sure exactly which portion of the finished script was done by which writer.

Everyone agrees that Mankiewicz should be credited with the search for Rosebud, and Welles said that he wished he could have written the dialogue where Bernstein talks about the girl in a white dress on the ferry. Beyond that, neither Welles nor Mankiewicz agree on who wrote what.

Mankiewicz said that his original idea was to tell a love story based on the long-running love affair between William Randolph Hearst, the owner of numerous newspapers including the "San Francisco Examiner," and Marion Davies, a Hollywood movie star of the 1930s.

Mankiewicz had been a guest of Hearst's at Hearst Castle at San Simeon and knew firsthand the kind of lavish parties and weekends that occurred there. Welles took that original idea and turned it into something different.

Mankiewicz said, perhaps somewhat cattily, that when he needed an inspiration for the egotistical Kane he would just pretend that it was the 25-year-old boy genius Welles that he was writing the scene for.

When the movie was completed, Hearst attempted to buy the negative from RKO so he could destroy it, but he was refused. Once the movie was released, none of Hearst's papers would accept advertising for the movie and his critics panned the movie at every opportunity.

In fairness to Hearst, though there are elements in the story that are based on his life, many other incidents are fiction or based on the lives of other wealthy tycoons.

For instance, Hearst's mistress Marion Davies was an accomplished movie star while McCormick, the owner of the "Chicago Tribune," had a mistress who tried without success to be an opera singer. Welles himself said that he had played a dirty trick on Hearst.

WELLES

From the time he could talk, Orson Welles was seen as a genius, a boy wonder. At age five, he was reading and reciting Shakespeare and complained bitterly if he was given the children's version of Shakespeare's plays instead of the adult text. By eight he knew most of Shakespeare's plays by heart.

Welles was born in Wisconsin to an affluent family. His mother moved in artistic circles, his father was a fun-loving playboy. They separated when Welles was young, and he spent a pampered childhood in the company of adults. He often traveled with his father and lived in luxurious hotels.

Rarely enrolled in school, Welles was mostly tutored at home. At 10, he entered a private school designed for the rich and gifted. He left at 15, ending his formal education.

Fueled by Shakespeare, Welles developed a passion for the stage at an early age. On his own at 16, he earned a living as an actor for one of the leading theatrical companies in Dublin.

Back in New York at 18, he quickly became a radio star as the voice of The Shadow, making a thousand dollars a week at a time when a loaf of bread was a dime. Using his lucrative salary, Welles produced innovative productions of Shakespeare in Harlem with an all-black cast. Critics loved them.

At 22, he founded his own company, the Mercury Theatre, to do stage and radio plays. That same year, his radio play based on H. G. Wells' Classic *War of the Worlds* became the stuff of legends. The broadcast, on April Fools Day, produced near panic on the East coast as many listeners thought that New Jersey had really been invaded by Martians. It also put Welles on the cover of *Time* magazine. He was 22 and famous.

Orson Welles had gone from nobody to the darling of radio and Broadway in a few short years. He was the boy genius. The boy wonder. The movies would be next.

At 24, Welles came to Hollywood filled with enthusiasm and optimism. Many of the actors and writers that he worked with in radio and on stage in New York came with him.

He called his contract with RKO studios the best erector set a boy ever had. In a short time, his brash manner got him into trouble in a Hollywood tightly controlled by the heads of a few powerful studios. In just a few more years, Orson Welles would outlive his welcome in Hollywood.

Orson Welles was 25 when he played Charles Foster Kane. It is an incredible acting tour de force. Welles' career, which started with so much promise, never fulfilled that promise.

He was fired from his next film, *The Magnificent Ambersons*, before it was completed. He was fired from a number of Hollywood films before they were completed.

For the next 20 years, Welles bounced back and forth between Hollywood and Europe, looking for financing for films. Many never got off the ground and none reached the heights of *Citizen Kane*.

He made some good films, such as *Touch of Evil* and *The Lady from Shanghai*, and there is a wonderful acting performance in *The Third Man*, but with Welles one is always left with the sense of promise unfulfilled. When one watches the 1957 studio version of *Touch of Evil* (Welles was fired before the film was completed) and compares it with the recent version re-cut to Welles' seventy page memo, one is struck by the subtle genius and command of Orson Welles.

Yet, Hollywood was a very difficult place for boy geniuses who wanted to do things their way. Welles wanted to push past the boundaries of genre entertainment, but Hollywood was about selling tickets, not artistic expression.

As one Hollywood executive said, "We are in the business of selling tickets, not making movies." Regrettably, Welles wanted to make movies that meant something. Instead, we are left with a sense of what might have been, or what if . . .

TRIVIA

The camera tends to look up at Charles Foster Kane and his best friend Jedediah Leland as a way of visually emphasizing their power importance while looking down at weaker characters like Susan Alexander Kane.

Xanadu's design is based on William Randolph Hearst's elaborate "Castle" in San Simeon and Mont St Michel in France.

Orson Welles chipped his anklebone halfway through production and had to direct for 2 weeks from a wheelchair. When he was called upon to stand up onscreen, he wore metal braces.

For the scenes featuring an older Kane, Orson Welles began make-up at 2:30 am to be ready for a 9:00 am start.

Though universally recognized as based roughly on the life of William Randolph Hearst, there were also elements in the story that applied to the life of Chicago utilities magnate Samuel Insull.

The original negatives of *Citizen Kane* were destroyed in a fire during the 1970s.

Editor Robert Wise dragged the "News on the March" negatives over concrete, among other tortures, to give them an aged look.

It was the head of RKO pictures who suggested the title change from "American" to "Citizen Kane." Orson Welles had also thought about calling the film "John Q."

Dorothy Comingore (Susan) was pregnant when shooting began. Welles hid her advancing condition by shooting her behind tables or by obscuring her body in flowing dressing gowns.

CHAPTER 10

THE STUDIO SYSTEM

Casablanca

Courtesy of the John Springer Collection/Corbis.

Casablanca is perhaps America's favorite film, with many filmgoers seeing the film over and over. *Casablanca* represents Hollywood studio system filmmaking at its peak. This is literally the best of what Hollywood had to offer in those golden years from the late 1920s to the end of the 1940s. How does an unproduced play written by two school teachers about their summer vacation become one of the most beloved films of all time? It is a long and twisted tale that illustrates how the Hollywood studio system worked.

A high school teacher and his wife visiting the South of France in the summer of 1938 saw firsthand the turmoil and confusion that the threat of war and the spread of Nazism caused in Europe. They used those experiences to create "Everybody Comes to Rick's." Though it was never produced as a play, it became the foundation for *Casablanca*, but there were many changes in story, theme, and ending before *Casablanca* reached the screen.

Warner Brothers optioned the play based on its similarity to other successful plays and films. Hollywood has always loved redoing successful things in new ways. To quote the story analyst who evaluated "Everybody Comes to Rick's," the play promised "sophisticated hokum, colorful characters, exotic locales, a tense love story, and suspense." These were the elements that Hollywood searched for, not innovation.

HOLLYWOOD STUDIO SYSTEM

In essence, the Hollywood studio system was a factory system. The studios controlled every aspect of film making from original material to financing, distribution and ownership of theaters. Every studio had offices in New York to arrange financing and offices around the world to distribute and market their films. Almost from the beginning, Hollywood has been an international enterprise. During the '20s and '30s, half of

Hollywood's revenue came from foreign markets and at times Hollywood controlled as much as 80 percent of the world's box offices.

At the height of their success, the studios were making 50 films a year or more. Musicals, westerns, gangster pictures or romantic comedies; whatever the genre, the most important element was the star. Each film story revolved around a main character—a star. And not just any star, but a specific persona. So *Casablanca* was tailored to Bogart, the tough loner, and Bergman, the ethereal beauty. Numerous writers were brought in to punch up the characters until they fit Bogart's and Bergman's personas.

The ending of the play was a particular problem. In the play, Rick sleeps with Ilsa, then gives her the letters of transit, shoots and kills major Strasser, then turns himself in and goes to jail. How many Hollywood films have you seen where the hero goes to jail and the film ends? Breaks out of jail . . . maybe, executed . . . maybe, quietly goes to jail . . . never.

The solution says a lot about screen writing as well as Hollywood film making and storytelling. As the story goes, the Epstein Brothers (identical twins) and many others were stumped by the ending. After weeks of massaging the script, suddenly one afternoon the twins looked at each other and said in unison, "Round up the usual suspects." That's a Hollywood story, so one can never be quite sure how accurate it is.

But notice how those words allow Capt. Renault to follow his conscience instead of his pocketbook and let Rick off the hook. Now both can rejoin the fight for freedom. Rick, rejuvenated by love, and Captain Renault with a new-found sense of patriotism, walk off and "begin a beautiful friendship." Now that is a Hollywood ending. It was love triumphant, patriotic, heroic, uplifting, energizing, and audiences loved it.

Different writers had different specialties. The Epstein brothers were brought in to add sparkle and wit with lines like: "Here's looking at you, kid." Others beefed up the role played by Claude Raines, fleshing out his off-beat friendship with Rick.

Rick was originally a married New York lawyer with three kids. He becomes a former gun runner with a nebulous past—but running guns to the right side.

Ilsa, played by Ingrid Bergman, was originally an American with loose morals and a talent for moving from man to man. In *Casablanca* she becomes almost saint-like, even as she is torn between her love for two men.

The producer was the key person in the studio system overseeing all script changes, as well as deciding who would star and who would direct. Hal Wallis, the executive in charge of *Casablanca*, produced more than 200 films in a career that spanned four decades. Studio executives and producers needed to be versatile. Hal Wallis produced some of the best films in a number of genres including westerns like *Stagecoach* and *True Grit,* musicals such as *Yankee Doodle Dandy* and Elvis' *Blue Hawaii*, detective films like *The Maltese Falcon* and the gangster classic *Little Caesar.*

Hal Wallis was particularly choosy about who would star. He had worked with Bogart on *The Maltese Falcon* and knew early on that he was right for the part, but the leading lady was a more difficult proposition. To get Ingrid Bergman for *Casablanca*, Wallis flew to New York, cornered David O. Selznick in his hotel and convinced him to trade Ingrid Bergman for Olivia de Haviland. The practice is not much different than two baseball owners trading ball players.

In the studio system, everyone was under long-term contract, even the stars. They did as they were told, or they did not work or get paid. As Clark Gable said, "It was a gilded cage that he lived in, but it was a cage."

Humphrey Bogart's background was quite different from his screen persona. The son of a successful Long Island doctor, he spent years on Broadway before Hollywood beckoned. After years of small parts in forgettable films, he finally got a chance at a starring role. Even then, it was years before he got the chance to play the tough guy roles that made him a star. *Casablanca* made Bogart a romantic leading man. It took Bogart more than 20 years to become Bogart.

Ingrid Bergman, a Swedish actress, was brought to America under a personal services contract as David O. Selznick's latest discovery. Selznick lent her out to various studios for more than he paid her.

Bergman's career took off after *Casablanca* and she became one of Hollywood's most desirable leading ladies. She was a personal favorite of Alfred Hitchcock.

The director of *Casablanca*, Michael Curtiz was considered Warner Brothers' best director. Like many Hollywood directors, he began his career in Europe A studio director par excellence, it didn't matter to him what kind of picture or who the stars were. He was a visual storyteller. His credits show his versatility. Westerns, musicals, action-adventure, film noir—it did not matter. The studios provided the scripts and he provided the visuals.

Originally from Hungary and an émigré himself, Michael Curtiz had perhaps a heightened awareness of the plight of the characters in *Casablanca*. Though he left Europe before the arrival of the Nazis, many of his family members had left Eastern Europe in similar fashion to the refugees in Rick's Place.

A number of actors in the film, like Peter Lorre who played Ugarte, also fled Europe ahead of the Nazis. Lorre had been a star in Germany before coming to America and enjoyed a long, successful career as a supporting actor in Hollywood.

It seems clear when viewing *Casablanca* that this film, like most studio films, is a melding of the genius of many people, with each area designed and executed by an expert; someone at the top of his craft. For instance, the set design and lighting combines to create a Morocco of the mind vs. a real Morocco. From the success of *Casablanca*, it seems that audiences also prefer Hollywood's version of heroism, patriotism, and beauty.

HISTORY

To understand *Casablanca* as audiences in the 1940s understood it, you must know what was going on in the world during the 1930s and early '40s.

First, it's important to realize that during the 1930s there was a significant isolationist movement in this country. Our experiences in World War I had convinced many Americans that we were better off letting the Germans, the English and the French fight their own wars. So, even though World War II started in 1939, it wasn't until the Japanese bombed Pearl Harbor in 1941 that the United States entered the war.

The evolution of Rick's character mimics U.S. involvement in the war. He starts off neutral and ends up joining the fight for freedom. There are numerous lines in the film like "that's a wise foreign policy" or "I stick my neck out for no one" that in context can be seen as pro war propaganda.

After the Germans conquered France, they partitioned the country down the middle, controlling Paris and eastern France while a pro-German, French government was installed in Vichy, a small town in southern France, to run the rest of the country. That's why after Bogart shot Captain Strasser and Captain Renault ordered his men to "round up the usual suspects," Captain Renault throws away the bottle of Vichy water.

The film was rushed into the theaters shortly after the allies had landed in *Casablanca*. This was serendipitous and Hollywood did not want to pass up any free publicity.

CHARACTER RAMP

Bogart's character in *Casablanca* is similar to many characters from the Hollywood film factories, as he goes from cynical selfish loner to committed optimistic Patriot. Hollywood loves this kind of character ramp.

Casablanca immediately spawned a number of successful takeoffs. In *To Have and Have Not*, there is Bogart, a piano player, a nightclub a lot like Rick's Place, a damsel in distress, and political intrigue.

Even later films like *Star Wars* owe a great deal to *Casablanca* with its storm troopers and love triangle. Woody Allen wrote a play, *Play it Again Sam* and then starred in the movie version where Bogart gives Woody Allen advice on dealing with women and Woody gets to relive the ending from *Casablanca*. *Casablanca* was updated in the '90s with Robert Redford in the Bogart role in the regrettably-dreadful *Havana*.

Though many have tried to duplicate the magic, the film that resonates with each new generation is *Casablanca*. We may not know the history, the actors, or the trivia, but we know what we like, and the Hollywood studio system knew how to create images that could last.

Casablanca and the 1940s mark the highpoint of the studio system. For many reasons, the '50s would be a time of steep decline until the studio system would collapse completely during the mid '60s. Movies today are made under a very different system. The studios today are, in essence, financing and distribution systems. Everyone else, writers, directors and actors, are free agents out on their own moving from studio to studio and film to film. This is the exact opposite from the old studio system where everyone was under contract and knew his place.

TRIVIA

Ingrid Bergman said that she had kissed Bogart but did not really know him. They didn't socialize. She said he was cordial, professional and helpful, but at the end of a day of shooting they went their separate ways.

Dooley Wilson, who played the piano player in the film, was in reality a drummer. Dooley only pretended to play the piano. Hollywood has never been about reality.

Dooley did sing "As Time Goes By" and made a lot of money off the recordings. The studio considered removing "As Time Goes By," a song popular in the early '30s, but by that time, Ingrid Bergman had already cut her hair for her next picture *For Whom The Bell Tolls* so they could not reshoot her scenes with Dooley.

Conrad Veidt, who played Major Strasser, left Germany not because he was Jewish but because he couldn't stand the Nazis. In Hollywood he had a long career playing Nazis on the screen.

Much of *Casablanca* was written as it was being shot, so Ingrid Bergman didn't know with whom she was going to end up at the end of the film. Many people think it added to her performance. In fact, the ending was written by the producer after filming was completed and everybody had to be brought back to shoot the final airport sequence.

CHAPTER 11
GENRE

The Palm Beach Story

Courtesy of Paramount/The Kobal Collection.

The Palm Beach Story is an example of a genre well developed, polished, at the height of its power, with many of the same elements that were in *It Happened One Night* but pushed, amplified and explored. *The Palm Beach Story* then is a delightful example of an existing genre, the screwball/romantic comedy developed during the 30s but refined and twisted by an evolving world view.

GENRE

Understanding what genres are and how they function is absolutely key to understanding how movies and particularly Hollywood works. Literally, genre just means a particular style or type of art form. For example, a western, sci-fi, horror, are examples of genres in film and literature. Each of these genres has specific conventions including generally similar plots, characters, locations and dilemmas. The details in the stories will change from book to book and film to film, but the loosely defined boundaries of the genre remains.

Genre is very useful way of organizing and defining most art. Music, painting, literature, film of course even magazines have very well defined genres. Genre is a very useful tool for audiences. It is how most people find the kind of book, music, TV program or film that they want. Audiences already know what they like. They just want a new, fresh version.

Most people do not like all movies. They like certain kinds of movies with certain kinds of stars. Hollywood has prospered and thrived mainly by producing popular genres over and over again. Each time with slightly different stories, twists or nuances. As the genre matures and social situations change and evolve, the genre adapts changes and evolves. So westerns made in the 1920s or the 1940s will have significantly different themes but the basic contours of the western will remain. As already mentioned, the western has faded away because many of the key elements of the genre are no longer meaningful for today's audience.

Romantic comedy on the other hand and many of the elements of screwball comedies of the 1930s are still popular today. No matter who you are and what your situation, most human beings want to love and be loved. What that means, how you find love what the role of the sexes are may change but the basic human need remains. So romantic comedies are popular and have been popular decade after decade.

Genres are also useful for writers and directors because the basic outlines of the story, plot, characters and underlying values have been predetermined. The art comes in how these basic building blocks are arranged and developed. In fact it is crucial that the plot is not completely original, but that the story is both familiar and yet different. That is the film needs to be different enough so that it is not a cliché or a copy but familiar enough so that audiences already have a reasonable idea of what to expect. Now the director, writer and actors can use that expectation as a departure point to make the film they have in mind. Then they can surprise, twist and delight the audience by manipulating the conventions of a well-established genre.

From almost the beginning Hollywood understood that the two best ways to market, advertise and reach their audience was to have stars and genres that audiences liked and wanted to see over and over again. Each film a little different, but not too different. Audiences like variations not surprises.

THE PALM BEACH STORY

is classic screwball comedy. The plot is simple: a woman decides to divorce the man she loves, a struggling entrepreneur, and marry a millionaire so that she can finance her husband's new project. The wife, with her good looks and sex appeal, has no trouble finding a rich suitor. The film is full of rich generous men who help her with no strings attached. One man, the "Weenie King," first gives money to the wife, then later to the husband to help him get his wife back.

Mixed among the visual gags and pratfalls is wonderful, witty dialogue. And with a surprise ending, a potentially unresolvable love triangle ends well. It is all here: the ditzy rich, sexual innuendo, the woman controlling men with her charms, off screen sex between married but potentially separating mates, and a fair amount of slapstick humor.

This is screwball comedy at its best and it is easy to see the inspiration that *It Happened One Night* provided. But it is also easy to see that something had changed in the eight years since the making of *It Happened One Night*. The mood of audiences in the country had changed. *The Palm Beach story* is funny yet cynical with none of the easy populist sentiments and imagery of *It Happened One Night*.

Times had changed. The Great Depression was about money, economics and financial loss but one could still keep faith in humanity. It was easy to see that the failures of the 1930s and the Great Depression were failures of economic systems and politics. People and their spirit still mattered. But World War II was different. The crimes against humanity were almost unimaginable, the scale mind boggling and with no one to blame but other human beings. An uneasy, almost lighthearted cynicism was much the fashion in audiences and film of the 1940s.

PRESTON STURGES

Though he came to the genre late, one of the masters of screwball comedy was Preston Sturges. Originally a Broadway writer and then Hollywood screenwriter before becoming a director, his career took off with a series of screwball comedies in the early '40s.

From 1940 to 1945, Sturges wrote and directed hit after hit—almost all screwball comedies. As the genre faded and postwar audiences developed new tastes, Sturges' career declined.

As has happened so often in Hollywood, a writer or director will catch the mood of a nation and rise to prominence. When the mood changes, it has been hard for many to adapt. The history of Hollywood is littered with great filmmakers who lost touch with their audiences. From being the toast of Hollywood in 1945, Sturges died broke and forgotten in 1959.

END OF THE GENRE

Screwball comedy faded fast after the end of WWII. By 1950, the genre was dead, killed by affluence and changing societal values. The nation was prosperous after WWII. The Great Depression was over and there was no need to see the rich as silly buffoons.

The silent era had been over for 20 years. New writers, directors and actors had grown up with sound and were less adept at visual humor.

Perhaps most importantly, society's view of women had changed. Women as sexually-savvy adversaries for men had changed from being funny to serious business. A new kind of woman was showing up on the nation's screen. She was cold, hard-hearted, beautiful and deadly. These were the femmes fatales of film noir.

Many of the comic women of the '50s were gorgeous airbrains like Marilyn Monroe and Jane Mansfield instead of bright beauties like Claudette Colbert and Carol Lombard.

Many filmmakers have tried to recapture the zany truth inherent in the best screw-ball comedy, but it is hard. Today, without the constraints of censorship, it is hard to keep the couples apart. As with most genres, it is hard to recreate a feeling and a mood after the world has moved on. We still enjoy the screwball comedies but have a hard time creating them.

C H A P T E R   12
FILM NOIR

Double Indemnity

Courtesy of Underwood and Underwood/Corbis.

The world of film noir is full of cheap crooks, gullible men, shady but beautiful double-crossing women and crimes gone bad. It is a world of passion, darkness and failure. Film noir were dark stories set in a dark world. Film noir was a new way for American film to look at life and simply reflected the unconscious mood of many filmmakers. It developed spontaneously and was a sensibility more than a genre.

THE ROOTS

Film noir grew organically from a number of sources. Pulp fiction provided many of the stories. Freud added the psychological motivation. WWII inspired the mood. German expressionism supplied the dark lighting. The fatalism came with many of the European directors. Combined, they became film noir.

During the '20s and '30s, a style of literature known as pulp or hard boiled fiction developed, which often featured petty criminals committing bumbling yet grisly crimes of passion and double cross.

This was the era of Dashiell Hammitt, a former Pinkerton detective, who wrote *The Maltese Falcon*. The novel features Sam Spade, a sleazy detective, an alluring woman who double crosses everyone, and a number of unsavory characters.

This was also when Raymond Chandler created his detective, Philip Marlowe, who survives all the shady women in his cases by refusing to be seduced.

During the 1930s and '40s, James Cain wrote *Double Indemnity* and *The Postman Always Rings Twice*, both about wives who get gullible men to murder their husbands.

These and other works of pulp fiction involving ugly crimes by seedy, smalltime crooks doomed to failure became the basis of many of the film noirs of the '40s.

Many of the directors of film noir were from Europe, mostly from Germany. They left with the rise of Hitler and brought to Hollywood a European sense of existentialism and fatalism.

These directors saw Europe devastated by two bloody wars in the span of 20 years. It left them with little of the optimism or faith in human nature that was common in American films.

Flashbacks became a common way of introducing this sense of hopelessness. By starting the film at the end and showing the characters' failure, nothing can change what has happened. The character's fate had already been decided, the only question for the audience is why.

In *The Killers*, Burt Lancaster, in his first film, calmly waits in his room for two hired gunmen to come and kill him. Why? Why doesn't he run? Why doesn't he fight back? He is young, strong, handsome and virile. Yet he waits passively, lying on his bed until the gunmen open his door and empty their revolvers into him. The rest of the film tells his story. In essence, a beautiful, double-crossing woman broke his heart and his spirit. This is the world of film noir.

In *The Killing*, an early film by Stanley Kubrick, we see a race track robbery go bad through a series of overlapping flashbacks similar to those in *Citizen Kane*. The fatal flaw in the plans is a double-crossing woman.

Capers that go wrong are common plot devices in film noir. At the time, the world was struggling for survival, threatened by communism, nazism, war and the atom bomb. It was an open question whether human beings were clever enough to solve their propensity for self-destruction or whether they were just smart enough to ensure their destruction.

In caper film after caper film, the characters are just smart enough to try for the brass ring and dumb enough to fail. They are often pushed over the edge by lust, inflamed by beautiful, double-crossing, heartless women. Spider Women and femmes fatales are consistent features of film noir. In film after film, it is the duplicity of woman that is fatal.

The 1940s was the time of Rosie the Riveter. Twelve million men out of a total population of 80 million were overseas fighting WWII. Women had taken their place in the work force. What would happen when the men returned? Would women give up their jobs, their economic and sexual freedom and gladly become homemakers again? These were scary questions with no clear answers.

The noirs of the 1940s are dark mirror images of the light, screwball comedies of the 1930s. The basics are quite similar. In both the film noirs and the screwball comedies the women were usually smarter than the men.

In both kinds of films, women used sex to attract men. The difference is that in the comedies the men end up married and in the noirs they end up destroyed.

From the beginning Hollywood had been known for happy sugarcoated endings with everyone living happily ever after. Now in the 1940s, film after film had a downbeat, unhappy ending and yet they did very well at the box office.

By some estimates roughly 25 percent of all the films made from the mid '40s to the mid '50s were noirs. Many are easy to recognize by their names. Titles like *Touch of Evil*, *The Killer's Kiss*, *The Naked City*, *Night and the City*, *Panic in the Streets*, and *Scarlet Street* conjure up the right mental images.

The look of film noir is dark, full of shadows and shadowy characters. This kind of lighting has its roots in German expressionism of the 1920s, which established a psychological tone with set design and lighting. Many noir directors, writers, cinematographers and technicians flourished in Germany during the heyday of expressionism. When they came to Hollywood, they brought their tastes with them.

Freud became popular in America in the '40s and noir borrowed heavily from his psychological palate. In noir after noir, characters are driven by obsession, irrational love or psychosis. In noir, love is often twisted and obsessive. It is not only sexual love. In *Mildred Pierce*, a mother's unselfish love for a rotten daughter leads to murder. In *Double Indemnity*, a surrogate son's rivalry with his father figure motivates a murder.

In the world of noir, the past often comes back to haunt the present. Once you make a mistake, there is no redemption. It may take awhile, but in noir, nobody gets away with anything. All transgressions, stupid mistakes and misplaced trust are punished. Even common, everyday actions can be deadly. In *DOA*, an innocent notary witnesses the signing of a document and is lethally poisoned. He spends the rest of the film trying to find out why. Ultimately, he discovers he was just in the wrong place at the wrong time.

Since noir is a state of mind more than a genre with conscious rules, a lot of film noirs have some of these elements but few have all of them. The writers and directors who created the noirs of the '40s were simply reflecting the dark unsettled mood of a nation at war. They did not know they were creating a new film style.

WWII saw millions of civilians killed, the methodical gassing and exterminating of whole populations in the Nazi death camps, and the dropping of atomic weapons on Japanese civilians.

French critics coined the term after WWII. Noir is a French word for black and this is the world of film noir, a black world of dark shadows, seedy characters and psychologically-damaged egos. There are noir detective movies, noir westerns, and even noir comedies.

During WWII, Hollywood's films were cut off from Europe. After the War, Hollywood shipped many of the earlier productions to Europe. French critics were astounded by the differences in pre- and post-war American films. In 1939, films like *Stagecoach*, *The Wizard of Oz*, and *Mr. Smith Goes to Washington* were full of optimism and heroics.

In the late '40s, there were numerous films like *Double Indemnity* credited by many as the first true film noir. *Double Indemnity* has it all. It is based on the pulp fiction novella by James Cain that fictionalizes an infamously tawdry murder of the late

'20s. The murderous lovers are driven by greed, fake passion, and a Freudian need by a surrogate son to outsmart the father figure.

The leading lady is cold hearted, calculating and, as she says of herself, "rotten to the core." The leading man kills his lover after killing her husband. What a pair. Their perfect crime unravels almost immediately. They are smart enough and bold enough to plot and commit a cold-blooded killing but not strong enough, loyal enough or smart enough to get away with it.

The film begins with a flashback as the murderous lover narrates how he went from a carefree, successful insurance agent to a double murderer with a bullet hole in him. All it took was ringing the wrong doorbell of an upscale home on a sunny afternoon.

There is no salvation for anyone at the close of the film. All we learn is that with the right bait, the right temptation or the right timing, any of us might be lured to our destruction.

BILLY WILDER

Billy Wilder, the director, was a leading screenwriter in Berlin before he left the rising tide of anti-Semitic Nazism for Hollywood. Remarkably, beyond a few phrases, he did not speak English when he got to America. Yet within a few short years, he was one of the leading writers at Paramount—often writing sparkling comedies of wit and irony.

His normal writing partner, Charles Brackett, a man with genteel Ivy League sensibilities, wanted nothing to do with *Double Indemnity*. It was too ugly and distasteful a story.

Wilder collaborated with Raymond Chandler, a leading writer of hardboiled fiction. The two did not get along. Chandler disliked the arrogant Wilder, did not like Hollywood and only did the film for the money. Wilder disliked the older, moralizing Chandler and had to continually force Chandler to conform to the peculiar needs of a screenplay.

Ironically, once the screenplay was completed, Wilder insisted that the studio pay for Chandler to be on the set every day of filming just in case scenes needed to be rewritten. Once the film was made, each acknowledged the genius of the other, but neither cared to work together again.

The screen writers made many changes to Cain's original book but remained faithful to the trashy tone. The screenplay was nominated for an Academy Award.

Billy Wilder was easily one of the best studio directors of the period. In a long and illustrious career, he made several other top-notch film noirs, *Sunset Boulevard* and *Ace in the Hole*, a number of excellent comedies, most notably *Some Like It Hot* and *The Apartment,* and an excellent prisoner of war film, *Stalag 17*. Each of these films had the distinctive bite that was Wilder.

Raymond Chandler preferred to write novels, although from time to time he was lured to Hollywood. He won an Academy Award for writing the screenplay for *The Blue Dahlia*, but many of his Hollywood writing associations were unpleasant, including a screenplay for *Strangers on a Train* that was almost completely thrown out by Hitchcock.

Several of his novels, most notably *The Big Sleep* and *Farewell My Lovely*, have been made and remade into films a number of times.

NOIR TODAY

Today, many filmmakers try to make films with the sensibilities of the early noirs. Yet it is hard to recreate a world of thoughts, ideas, fears and concerns, once the original conditions have evolved and mutated into a new set of fears and concerns. Often, the neo noirs of today are nastier, more violent, darker and more sexually explicit than the originals. Yet somehow when empty nihilism is exchanged for the rich fatalism found in the noirs of the '40s, a crucial ingredient is gone. We are left with the crimes and ugliness but no underlying existential sense of truth about the twists and turns of life.

TRIVIA

At first, Fred MacMurray wanted nothing to do with *Double Indemnity*. He had been working mostly in light comedies and was afraid it would ruin his career. Yet, probably his two best film roles are with Wilder, where he plays against type in *The Apartment* and *Double Indemnity*.

Barbara Stanwyck wanted very much to play the coldhearted Phyllis Dietrichson in *Double Indemnity*.

Some critics complained that the film was a recipe for murder, but the film was able to meet the Production Code since justice is served at the end.

The film has been redone several times and the remakes hold up well. *Body Heat* with Kathleen Turner and William Hurt is an excellent '80s version and *The Last Seduction* is a small-budget independent '90s version.

Each generation adds its own twists to the basic story but they all have their roots in *Double Indemnity*.

There have been many attempts to recreate the world of noir in later generations of films. *Chinatown* is an excellent '70s noir in the Raymond Chandler tradition. *Blade Runner* is a sci-fi version of noir. *After Hours* by Scorsese is a dark comedy in a subtype sometimes called yuppie noir.

Many of the original noirs were low budget B pictures done by young directors on the way up. The dark lighting hid cheap sets, and attitude and style could supplant polished scripts and accomplished actors.

Blood Simple, by the Coen brothers, and *Shallow Grave*, an English version of yuppie noir, are part of an ongoing tradition of low budgets and film noir.

CHAPTER 13
BLACKLISTING

The Front

Courtesy of Columbia/The Kobal Collection.

Just when Hollywood had it made, it all fell apart. The late '40s were Hollywood's best years at the box-office. By the early '50s box-office receipts had dropped 50 percent. For Hollywood, a number of calamities happened almost simultaneously. The biggest was the coming of free home entertainment—television. The movies had survived and even thrived with the coming of radio, but TV would be different. On a graph you can plot rising television sales right along side plummeting box-office receipts. TV's impact was dramatic but many other events conspired to spell the end of the studio system.

During WWII people flocked to the cities to work in the war industry. They worked long, hard hours, made lots of money and went to the movies an average of three times a week. At the end of the war, they moved to the suburbs, started families and stopped going to the movies.

After the war, the studios were forced to sell off their theaters as part of the settlement of an anti-trust suit by the federal government. Now the studios would have to compete to show their movies. They no longer had guaranteed outlets for their films.

The post-war era was a time of unionization in this country and in Hollywood. Salaries for everyone who worked behind the camera went up substantially.

Surprisingly, global politics and the Cold War contributed heavily to the studio system's demise.

COLD WAR/BLACKLISTING

Just when Hollywood needed its best writers and storytellers, many were blacklisted—prevented from working by politics.

The Red Scare of the late '40s and early '50s is an understandable but sad chapter in American history. At the end of WWII, almost immediately the glow of victory over

Germany and Japan was doused by the start of the Cold War with Russia. Even worse, in the late '40s Russia quickly demonstrated the ability to build atom and then hydrogen bombs and China fell to the communists and Mao. The domino theory, where one country after another might go communist, seemed plausible. Then, in the early '50s, in a surprise attack North Korea almost overran South Korea, and we were in a shooting war with the communists.

As a result of all these external political pressures, a witch hunt for communists and communist sympathizers began in this country. It was an understandable but ultimately silly hysteria.

It seems incredible today that many people were worried that the resolve of this nation could be undermined by the movies—that communist propaganda could be embedded in film and subliminally alter the nation's political will. Congressional committees were formed to investigate the possibility that Hollywood was being used to promote communism. The idea seems ludicrous today, but the repercussions were tragic and real for the people caught in the vortex of the mass political hysteria of the 1950s.

The history is complicated. Many of the writers in Hollywood who were blacklisted were communists or at least quite liberal, but that was not a crime. During the Great Depression, many intellectuals and politicians thought that the future belonged either to the fascist or to the communists. The democracies in America, France and England seemed powerless to either solve the Great Depression or to stand up to the fascists, and communism seemed the lesser of the two evils.

Not all, by any means, but many who helped organized labor unions and strikes during the Great Depression were communists. But during the '30s, communism was not seen as a political threat. When we entered into the war in 1941, Russia became an ally. FDR literally called up Hollywood studio heads and asked them to make movies that would show Russia in a positive light. Hollywood was happy to oblige. But after the war, circumstances were different. Now those who supported communist or left-wing causes were under suspicion.

The opening shots in the war between Hollywood and Congress were fired by the House Un-American Activities Committee (HUAC). In 1947, a group of leading leftist writers, producers and directors were the first subpoenaed to testify in Washington. The Hollywood Ten, as they later became known, came to the hearings and debated with the committee but refused to testify or answer questions. The Hollywood Ten did not take the Fifth claiming protection from self-incrimination but the first, claiming that Congress was impeding their rights to free assembly and speech. The House Committee found them in contempt of Congress and adjourned.

The Hollywood Ten appealed to the courts. Several years later, the Supreme Court rejected their last appeal and 10 leading Hollywood writers, producers and a director went to jail for terms from six months to a year. Imagine, several Academy Award-winning writers went to jail in a conflict with Congress over civil rights. Hard to imagine that happening today.

During the early '50s the House Un-American Activities Committee called leading members of Hollywood to testify about communists in Hollywood. Top directors, actors, writers and studio heads all came to Washington. Nobody was exempt. You could refuse to testify under the Fifth Amendment protection against self-incrimination and not go to jail, but you would be blacklisted.

BLACKLISTING

The blacklist became a way of life in Hollywood in the '50s; this is how it worked. Those who were called to testify and took the Fifth could not work at any major studios. Those who testified and named names, informing on the people they knew who had supported various leftist causes by marching in parades, signing petitions, making contributions, or attending meetings, were able to work. Those who refused to testify, didn't work. Many, many of Hollywood's best writers refused to name names and their careers were over.

The House Committee's reason for asking people to name names was not to develop new leads and information. In most cases, the committee knew who had been involved. They simply wanted the publicity that came with having important, highly-visible Hollywood personages testify publicly.

The interesting thing is that being a communist and certainly contributing money to organizations like the American Civil Liberties Union was never illegal. Blacklisting is illegal, so although everyone in Hollywood knew there was a blacklist, all the studios denied it. Those who were blacklisted were not told they were blacklisted. They were just told they were not right for the assignment or the role. And it was difficult to defend against something everyone denied existed.

The blacklisting was enforced by the threat of economic boycott. Organizations like the American Legion threatened to boycott and set up picket lines at the box-office of any movie that used any unrepentant leftist sympathizer. It did not matter whether they were actors, writers, directors, producers or in any of the crafts behind the camera.

The political climate of the '50s changed the very stories that Hollywood could do. For instance, no film that looked at problems of race relations or poverty could be made during the early '50s. This was not because of overt censorship but because such stories painted a negative picture of America. America was in a propaganda war with the Soviet Union. How America was portrayed on the screen was seen as critically important in this global struggle for the hearts and minds of the uncommitted nations of the world. As a result, the '50s is one of the most vapid decades in American cinema.

So, at a time when Hollywood was struggling with declining box-offices, it was difficult to produce stimulating entertainment. In the 1950s, it was simply too dangerous to be artistically adventuresome. Instead Hollywood relied on old tired formulas, vapid comedies, big-budget musicals and grand biblical epics to compete with television.

After blacklisting faded away in the late 1960s, the kinds of films made in Hollywood changed dramatically. *Midnight Cowboy*, the Academy Award winner for the best picture in 1968, was written by Waldo Salt, a blacklisted writer. *MASH*, 1970, was written by Ring Lardner Jr., one of the Hollywood Ten. These kinds of films were not made during the '50s because risky projects that threatened to provoke controversy were simply not made.

THE FRONT

The Front plays as a comedy but most of the material is based on real events involving real people. The director Martin Ritt, writer Walter Bernstein, and actors Zero Mostel and Herschel Bernardi were blacklisted in the '50s. This was one of the few films that Woody Allen has done that he neither wrote nor directed. Woody Allen was never blacklisted but felt strongly about the subject matter.

Hollywood has made a few films touching on blacklisting besides *The Front. Guilty by Suspicion* with Robert DeNiro is an accurate dramatic telling of the story. There are several documentaries such as *Point of Order, The Weavers: Wasn't That a Time* and *Seeing Red* that capture the insane flavor of McCarthyism and the red hysteria of the '50s. But in general, Hollywood has ignored its lack of courage and ignoble behavior during the 1950s. Yet even today in Hollywood, there is still a great deal of animosity lying just below the surface.

In 1999, the director of *On the Waterfront*, Elia Kazan, received a lifetime achievement award from the Academy. His nomination was controversial and provocative because in 1953, this Oscar-wining director named names and annoyed almost everyone in Hollywood. He annoyed the right because he would not apologize for supporting communist causes in the '30s, and he annoyed the left because he did not denounce the public witch hunt of the '50s.

THE COMING OF TELEVISION

In the '50s television was the hot new medium. TV was willing to try new things to tell ignored stories and to give new talent a chance. Things have changed. Today broadcast television is ruled by ratings and its audience has been fractured by cable and the Internet, making it quite conservative. But, in the beginning, television could be quite innovative. Young new writers and directors were given the opportunity to show what they could do. Many of the next decades' best film directors, writers and actors got their start in television.

Stanley Kubrick was about the only new film director of note to start making movies for the studios in the early '50s. He started as an independent and quickly fled the rigidity of the studio system for England.

Television had a number of indirect effects on the movie industry. At first the Hollywood studios tried to ignore television. Later the studios realized they could make money by producing television series and selling their movies to the networks.

Color became common in the movies in part because of the development of color TV. Excellent quality color film had been around since the '30s. Big-budget features like *Gone with the Wind*, *The Wizard of Oz* and *Robin Hood* were produced in gorgeous Technicolor, but still most movies were shot in black-white.

Audiences did not seem to care whether films were in black-white or in color. So, the studios continued to make most films in black and white until they realized that their movies would be worth more to the television networks in color than in black and white.

Perhaps the greatest lasting impact television had on the movies was by indirectly encouraging Hollywood to introduce new widescreen formats like Cinemascope and Panavision. Hollywood developed these widescreen formats to attract audiences. They were designed to give the viewer an experience that was different from anything television could offer. Television is the shape it is because it closely mimicked the standard Hollywood screen format of the 1940s. When Hollywood went to widescreen format for many of its movies, they no longer fit the TV screen.

Today we have come full circle. New television standards for high definition digital television scheduled for 2008 have a widescreen format so that movies do not have to be letterboxed to be shown the way movie audiences see them.

The '50s were a difficult decade for the movies. Each year the audience dwindled. Movies had lost their magic. The old studio system could not adapt to the changing world of the '50s and '60s and was slowly fading away. Just when it seemed that movies and Hollywood would become irrelevant, new filmmakers, making movies in new ways for a new audience, would lead Hollywood into a renaissance of prosperity and influence, but the old studio system was gone.

TRIVIA

The director Martin Ritt; writer Walter Bernstein; and actors Zero Mostel, Herschel Bernardi, Lloyd Gough and Joshua Shelley, all were blacklisted during the 1950s.

This is one of the few films starring Woody Allen that he didn't write or direct.

C H A P T E R   14

THE 1950s

On the Waterfront

Courtesy of the John Springer Collection/Corbis.

*O*n the Waterfront is easily one of the best films of the 1950s—certainly one of the best films not directed by someone named Hitchcock or Wilder. In 1998 the American Film Institute ranked *On the Waterfront* as one of the top 10 films ever made. Yet, it is exactly the kind of film that Hollywood resisted making during the 1950s. Even though the film was highly profitable ($900,000 budget, $10,000,000 box office return) there were few films with the kind of realism offered in *On the Waterfront* made during the 1950s. Realism would not come to Hollywood— and with it a resurgence in the box office—until the 1960s.

For many reasons, Hollywood preferred to make light escapist entertainment during the 1950s. Not that the Hollywood studios had ever ventured far into social criticism during the preceding decades, but the 1950s were a time of particularly shallow, vapid films.

By the time *On the Waterfront* was made, Hollywood was in a terrible bind. Beginning in the late '40s, every year fewer and fewer tickets were sold. Every year, fewer and fewer people went to the movies. Their audience was evaporating. The impact of television had been immediate and substantial. Hollywood's response was to try to make films grander and bigger or slicker and more polished than anything on TV. What the movies did not want to do was to make films that had social bite or criticized American capitalism. Hollywood preferred safe formulistic genres because they were scared silly that controversial films would frighten off the dwindling audience they had.

Just as important, Hollywood films were recognized as crucial propaganda in the cold war with communism. The America presented by Hollywood was rich in material wealth and in personal freedom. It did not matter that segregation and separate but equal was still the way of life and the law of the land, or that there were tremendous areas of rural and urban poverty for both black and white in this country. What mattered was how

America looked on film. The world loved Hollywood films and their images of a wealthy American Shangri-La.

Hollywood was also constrained by the increasingly silly limits of censorship imposed by the Production Code. In the 1950s, officially and legally, America was still puritanical in its views. Homosexual sex and marriage outside of one's race was against the law in most states. Public obscenity could be and often was criminally prosecuted. Yet the Kinsey report published in 1948 showed that Americans at the time had a wide and voracious appetite for sex. But sex as it was lived by its audience would not come to Hollywood during the 1950s.

Not only was the content and storyline of most Hollywood films far removed from reality, but most films were shot on a soundstage. They were visual fantasy worlds to go with the sugar-coated realities that were the substance of most films of this era. These films might be fun, they might be attractive but in a superficial way. Hollywood movies of the '50s simply did not reflect how people lived, what their concerns were, or where they lived.

On the Waterfront is different. It was about something that was real. Starting in the late 1940s, Congress had been actively investigating Waterfront corruption. Many of the hearings were broadcast live on television. Waterfront corruption, kickbacks and bribes were front-page news. The film was shot on location, in a dramatic but realistic style. The story was about regular people caught up in the difficulties of earning a living and surviving.

Marlon Brando as Terry Malloy is not a heroic, larger-than-life character. He is a small-time guy who lost his one shot at being "somebody." His romantic interest, Eva Marie Saint, is certainly attractive, but in a small mousy sort of way. She certainly is not physically attractive like Marilyn Monroe, nor does she exude overt sexual energy. The couple walking together would turn no heads. Their ambitions are small. Brando just wants a few extra "potatoes," Eva Marie Saint to be a school teacher. Even these small dreams are difficult along the Waterfront, but they are the dreams and concerns of much of America during the 1950s.

STRUCTURE

The story and structure of the film is classic Hollywood storytelling, but with some significant twists. The hero of the film is not particularly bright or handsome. The hero is not asked to be tougher, smarter, faster with a gun or slicker than the crooks. He is simply asked to testify in court about the ugly corruption and murder that he knows are part of the Waterfront. He is asked to be an informer, to be Benedict Arnold, to turn on his former friends and his brother. Why? Because it is the right thing to do. This simple-minded clarity is what gives the film much of its punch.

Unlike many Hollywood films, the romance in *On the Waterfront* moves the story forward. It is fundamental to the drama and is not merely grafted on to generate box office potential. The underlying conflicts inherent in the story come to a head precisely because of the romance.

It is interesting to note that one of the leading actors, Lee J. Cobb, the screenwriter, Bud Schulberg, and the director, Elia Kazan, were "friendly" witnesses who named names in the McCarthy witch hunts of the early 1950s. Many in the Hollywood community who suffered because of the blacklisting thought that naming names was at best a cowardly action that justified the blacklisting and at worst was despicably self serving. Certainly this is one of the few Hollywood films where testifying against your former friends is considered the heroic thing to do. Even then, Marlon Brando becomes an outcast after he testifies. The audience understands why he testified and why his ostracism is unjustified. But even in *On the Waterfront*, Brando does not win approval by testifying but by taking the Union mob on with his fists.

METHOD ACTING

The acting on the waterfront is notable. Many of the leading actors had been trained in the method style, which simply means that the actors try to internalize the feelings and emotions to become the character they are portraying. The Method style at the time was outside the Hollywood norm, where actors were usually chosen for their screen presence and amiable good looks. Most Hollywood stars simply create a persona and then portray that image over and over again. But Brando, Lee J. Cobb, Karl Malden, Eva Marie Saint, and Rod Steiger all created characters that had a life of their own. Particularly, the Terry Malloy of Marlon Brando is his unique creation. One has only to think of the film that might have been made if Frank Sinatra had been cast in the Brando role as Elia Kazan had originally suggested.

BRANDO

Marlon Brando was the first method actor to fundamentally alter Hollywood film. For many, he defined method acting. Originally from Omaha, he moved to New York to study at the Actors Studio with Stella Adler. From early on, there was something electric and special about his presence on stage. He resisted coming to Hollywood because he was reluctant to sign the standard seven-year contracts of the era that gave the studios absolute control over an actor's roles and career. Many of the actors to follow, Paul Newman, Steve McQueen, Jack Nicholson, Robert DeNiro, and Al Pacino all cite Brando's overwhelming influence.

KAZAN

Before coming to Hollywood, Elia Kazan was an acclaimed Broadway director. He had already made a number of good to great films before *On the Waterfront*. During his career, he won two Academy Awards for directing and a number of Tony Awards. He received a lifetime achievement award from the Academy of Motion Pictures Arts and Sciences in 1998. Kazan was a controversial figure because, like many in the New York theater world of the 1930s, he was a communist. Kazan later became an anti-communist and during the '50s reluctantly named names about his associates of those 1930s theater days. Many never forgave him for testifying.

TRIVIA

A number of the actors who portrayed union gangsters were former prize fighters. Three, Tony Galento, Tami Mauriello and Abe Simon each fought Joe Louis for the heavy weight title and, of course, lost.

The film was shot in Hoboken, New Jersey.

The scene where Eva Marie Saint drops her glove and Marlon Brando picks it up and puts it on his hand was unplanned. During rehearsal, she dropped her glove accidentally and Brando improvised the rest.

The leading characters were based on real people: Terry Malloy was based on longshoreman and whistle-blower Anthony De Vincenzo; Father Barry was based on waterfront priest John M. Corridan; Johnny Friendly was based on mobster Albert Anastasia.

CHAPTER 15

CLASSICAL HOLLYWOOD STYLE

Rear Window

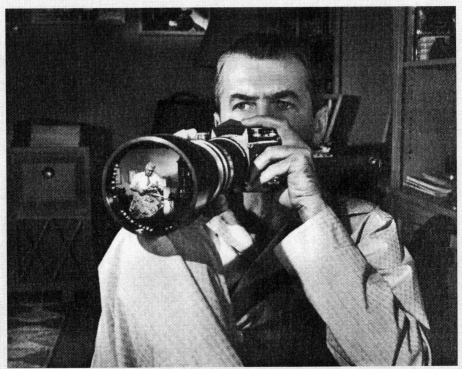

Courtesy of Bettman/Corbis.

Alfred Hitchcock is probably the most esteemed and copied filmmaker of the 20th Century. Filmmaker after filmmaker cites Hitchcock as the director they admire most. Filmmakers on both sides of the Atlantic from Scorsese and Spielberg to Lucas and Truffaut look at the ease and elegance of Hitchcock's work and see a master at the top of his craft.

From the '20s to the '60s, Hitchcock made wonderful films. Decade after decade in America and England, on his own or for the Hollywood studios, he made great films. Starting in the black and white silent era and ending with wide screen color, Hitchcock knew cinema and audiences. Other directors recognize his genius.

HITCHCOCK

Alfred Hitchcock was born at the turn of the century in Victorian England. Growing up, he was shy and chubby if not downright portly. In his first job, he worked for a catalog company drawing lighting and electrical fixtures. Artistic and technical by nature, he read industry film publications where he noticed that a Hollywood film company was coming to England to make movies. Hitchcock offered his services as an artist drawing illustrations for the title cards used in silent cinema. Once hired, he quickly moved from job to job and task to task until he was directing. By the late '20s, he was considered one of England's best directors.

He said that he was 22 years old before he ever had a glass of beer or a date. He married Alma, his editor at the studio, and together they formed a life-long partnership. She often advised him on story and scripting though remaining discreetly in the background.

One of Hitchcock's first films, *The Lodger,* is based on the infamous killer Jack the Ripper. The distributor found the film too arty and disturbing to release. After a protracted struggle, the film was released and audiences loved it. Hitchcock had found his niche. By the '30s, Hitchcock was easily the leading English director and considered a master of suspense. For newer audiences that have only seen *Psycho*, most do not realize that Hitchcock was not about horror and the macabre. Most of his films are full of suspense mixed with romance.

Hitchcock came to Hollywood in 1939, on a personal services contract to David O. Selznick. Selznick developed the projects while Hitchcock directed.

Their first collaboration, *Rebecca*, won the Academy Award for best picture but not for Hitchcock, the director. This was the last Hitchcock picture to receive an Academy Award and he never won a best director Academy Award. Late in his career, he was given a lifetime achievement award by the Academy.

For most of his career, Hitchcock was dismissed by critics as a facile director of popular entertainment but not really a serious director. The kinds of films he chose to make, spy chase films or psychological murder mysteries that often blend murder, humor and romance, most critics saw as so much fluff. Popular? Yes. Well-crafted? Yes. Serious? Weighty? No.

The French were the first to recognize the genius that was Hitchcock. Looking at the totality of his work, they noticed a consistency in theme, substance and visual images. French New Wave directors like Truffaut and Godard lavished praise on Hitchcock. He was honored by French film societies long before he was recognized in America, his adopted country. The French New Wave directors loved how simply and visually Hitchcock could tell a story. It was these abilities that later attracted American directors like Scorsese and Spielberg. They were particularly drawn to Hitchcock's ability to turn mundane inanimate objects into vibrant visual metaphors.

In *Notorious*, Ingrid Bergman steals her husband's keys to the wine cellar, then gives them to Cary Grant. The keys become a phallic symbol that represents many layers of treachery. At a party that night, a few bottles of champagne chilling in a tub of ice become a ticking clock—a dramatic, symbolic time bomb. When the champagne runs out, the husband will go to the wine cellar for more and find his wife, Ingrid Bergman, and Cary Grant, a U.S. agent, poking through evidence of his clandestine life as a supporter of a secret Nazi movement. Hitchcock cuts back and forth from the search in the wine cellar to the champagne-drinking party goers, building suspense. The scene climaxes with the husband looking for his missing key and realizing that his wife is an American spy and in love with Cary Grant. He has been betrayed at every level. All this from a few bottles of champagne and some keys on a key ring. Other filmmakers love this kind of simplicity.

Filmmakers also admired the emotional content that Hitchcock created with the camera. For *Vertigo*, Hitchcock invented a camera shot to mimic the feeling of vertigo. The camera dollies out as the lens zooms in, distorting spatial relationships.

Spielberg used this shot in *Jaws* when the sheriff roams the beach, looking for the great white shark while oblivious swimmers frolic in the surf, to convey the sheriff's mental vertigo.

In *Notorious*, there is a famous shot where Ingrid Bergman and Cary Grant are locked in an embrace passionately nibbling on each other's lips while the camera circles dizzily. The circling camera perfectly captures the intoxicated mood of the couple and nibbling is much more erotic than any passionate clench would be. This shot has been used by so many following filmmakers that today it has become a visual cliché.

Censorship at the time of *Notorious* would not allow for lengthy, passionate kisses. Hitchcock found a way around the censorship while remaining true to the scene and actually heightened the sexuality of the moment. Other filmmakers were impressed.

Over and over in Hitchcock films, one sees the same basic elements. His villains are generally educated, well-spoken and respected members of society like diplomats, professors, art dealers, successful businessmen, tennis pros, or motel owners. Only they often have a double-life as spies, murderers, or both.

Hitchcock's heroes are often flawed. Some literally, like Jimmy Stewart in *Vertigo*, who is afraid of heights. Or in *Rear Window* where he is something of a voyeur peering into other people's apartments with binoculars and high-powered lenses.

The women are beautiful and difficult, smart and head-strong, an obstacle to be overcome and an absolutely crucial ally to the hero. In *Notorious*, *The 39 Steps*, *The Man Who Knew Too Much,* and many others, it is the woman who finds out the essential information without which the hero would be doomed to failure.

For Hitchcock, men and women have to work as a team to succeed even though they have conflicting motives and rightly distrust each other.

Danger for Hitchcock lurks not in the mean street of the big city late at night, but in broad daylight in public—at the Statue of Liberty, Mount Rushmore, the movies or the symphony, on a train, answering a page at a fancy hotel or checking into the wrong motel. All can lead to danger and death in a Hitchcock film.

Usually, police are part of the hero's problems. Often they want to put him in jail for crimes he has not committed or do not believe a crime has been committed at all.

Directors with Hitchcock's consistency have led to an idea, called the Auteur theory. Auteur is simply a French word for author and means that though many people contribute to the making of the film it is the director's sensibilities and choices that ultimately shape the film.

REAR WINDOW

Rear Window is Hitchcock at his best. The movie opens with a tracking shot that starts on a thermometer, showing how steaming hot it is and then pulls back to reveal a framed photograph of a racing car crashing at the moment of impact. Flying towards the camera is one of the race car's wheels, looming large in the foreground moments before impact.

The tracking shot continues to show a crushed camera and then a framed negative next to a stack of a national magazine with the positive on the cover. Next comes Jimmy Stewart, sleeping in a wheel chair, in a body cast from his hip to the toes of one leg. In just a few visual seconds, Hitchcock establishes how Jimmy Stewart was injured and what his profession is.

On one level, *Rear Window* is a murder mystery. Did one of the tenants in the apartment building murder his nagging wife? One day she is there and the next day she is gone and her husband is washing knives and saws and cleaning the bathtub.

Was she murdered? Can Jimmy Stewart prove it? The police are no help and he is trapped in a wheel chair.

The film is also a romance. Grace Kelly wants Jimmy Stewart, but Jimmy Stewart wants to roam the world as a photographer and has no intention of settling down.

So the film has two questions: Can Jimmy Stewart prove there was a murder? And can Grace Kelly convince Jimmy Stewart that she belongs in his life on a permanent basis?

The solution: Grace Kelly becomes Jimmy Stewart's legs and alter ego. She is the one that breaks into the suspected murderer's apartment and finds the crucial evidence, a woman's wedding ring. When cornered, she puts the ring on her own finger to get it out of the apartment.

Symbolically, this act leads toward her own marriage to a formerly-reluctant and now admiring Jimmy Stewart. How elegant. In the other apartments, we are treated to different insights into marriage, relationships or the pitfalls of being single.

Miss Lonely Hearts contemplates suicide because she is alone. Miss Torso juggles wolves while she waits for her short dumpy serviceman lover to return home to her and her refrigerator. During the course of the film, a newly-wed goes from demanding lover to nagging wife. Across the courtyard, a middle-aged dog-loving couple live their lives in harmony.

For Hitchcock, marriage is an unpredictable gamble. The future may be domestic bliss, may be murder or may be just bickering, nagging and conflict.

At the end of *Rear Window*, Grace Kelly gives up her designer dresses for jeans and penny loafers. She is reading *Beyond the High Himalayas*. When she sees that Jimmy Stewart is peacefully asleep, she goes back to reading a fashion magazine. That scene sums up visually Hitchcock's thoughts on women, marriage, and relationships.

Rear Window is how Hitchcock sees the world. Danger can be as close as a husband. An innocuous jewelry salesman can be a cold-blooded killer, who dismembers his wife in the bathtub, distributes her body parts in the local rivers and keeps her head in a hat box. The police are going to be little help, and your girlfriend—as much as she loves you—has her own ideas. Hitchcock's consistency makes him one of the leading auteurs in the history of filmmaking as well as telling us something about what audiences want in their movies.

Hitchcock is a good example of a director who could work well with the Hollywood studios without losing his personal artistic point of view. Unlike Orson Welles, who continually fought with the studios and lost, Hitchcock, though he had his battles, was happy to make the kinds of films the studios wanted.

Hitchcock wanted to make entertaining films. He saw himself as an entertainer, not as an artist. He said that if he could hook up the audiences to wires and control their emotions, he wouldn't have to make films.

Hitchcock has influenced so many filmmakers in so many parts of the world that it is difficult to conceive of a world of cinema without his films.

TRIVIA

With his droll wit and a hint of the dark side in his persona, Hitchcock was an interesting man and a few stories are useful in understanding his films. As always, when one is relating a Hollywood story, one must remember that Hollywood has little regard for letting truth get in the way of a good tale.

An interviewer once asked Hitchcock if he had said that actors were like cattle. Hitchcock said no, what he had said was that actors should be treated like cattle. He is also quoted as having said that he envied Disney with his cartoon characters because Disney did not have to put up with actors.

Yet Hitchcock was fussy about his cast and stars. He said that when he wanted an everyman he would cast Jimmy Stewart, when he wanted someone every man wanted to be he cast Cary Grant. He made four films with each and both would commit to any Hitchcock project long before a script was available.

He never did find suitable replacements when both Stewart and Grant became too old to play the romantic lead, though he tried some of the best actors around, like Sean Connery and Paul Newman.

When Grace Kelly retired, Hitchcock shelved a project though the script was completed, and never made the film.

Hitchcock also had a perverse sense of humor that came out in his films and in his dealing with actors. He did not get along with Kim Novack, the star of *Vertigo*, and said that he took a great deal of pleasure in having her repeat over and over the scene where she jumps into the frigid waters of San Francisco Bay.

The way Hitchcock liked to work was to tell his writer what was going to happen and where. The writer's job was to know why the characters were there and what they were going to do next.

For example, Hitchcock knew that he wanted Cary Grant to be attacked by a crop duster in a cornfield in *North by Northwest,* but he had no idea why Cary Grant was there and where he was going to next. That was the writers' job.

Supposedly, Hitchcock napped through the filming of the shower scene for *Psycho*. He had everything drawn out ahead of time in storyboards as he often did. He was content to let the graphic artist say action and cut. He had already made all the important decisions and the filming was just a detail.

CHAPTER 16

SEX IN THE 1950s

Pillow Talk

Courtesy of Universal/The Kobal Collection.

illow Talk is exactly the kind of film that Hollywood wanted to make during the 1950s. It is full of light romance, glib humor, funny situations and attractive stars. Based on classic formulas, it made a lot of money, was nominated for five Academy Awards and won for best screenplay. *Pillow Talk* is still fun today; the only trouble with it is that it is about nothing. It is all surface. The situations are simply unbelievable. Not that Hollywood stories or characters need to be believable, but in the Hollywood films of the '30s and '40s grains of realism were at least mixed in with the fantasy. *Pillow Talk* is all cotton candy.

From story to images, it is an imagined world. The lighting for the film is bright, studio lighting with none of the personality and texture of the real world. The sets themselves are spacious and lovely but unreal. Though located in New York City, one of the most culturally- and ethnically-diverse cities of the world, the film has only white actors including the extras walking on the street. The only African American actors in the film are musicians—a common occurrence in Hollywood films of the '50s.

ANALYSIS

By 1959 this was the Hollywood ideal: make beautiful, clever films with box office stars that had no content. The only reason this is important is to show the path that Hollywood was pursuing in the face of a continually dwindling box office. For over a decade now, Hollywood had sold fewer tickets every year than the preceding year. There is nothing wrong with this kind of superficial entertainment. What is important is how quickly Hollywood would change in the 1960s. Realism, content, films about something would be the antidote for Hollywood's lack of inspiration during the 1950s. Powered by a renewed sense of realism Hollywood style, the mid '60s begin a time of box office growth. In 1959 *Pillow Talk* is the best the old Hollywood studio system could produce. The new Hollywood would be quite different. In 1959, Hollywood is on the verge of nothing less then revolutionary change.

1959

The world of 1959 was a world on the edge of change. The civil rights movement was beginning to gather steam. The women's movement had started. The coming of the pill would change sexual mores almost overnight. The threat of global nuclear war was real. The threat of communism seemed real to many. In 1959 Castro took over in Cuba and the Russian premier, Khrushchev, came to the United Nations and announced he would "bury" us. Satellites already orbited the earth, and men would soon follow. The 1960s would be a very different world and Hollywood would make very different kinds of films.

THE INFLUENCE OF EUROPEAN TRENDS—1959

In France and England, new, young directors began shooting simple stories on location about real people. In France, these kinds of films were called New Wave, in England, Kitchen Sink cinema. Often shooting handheld with available light, they brought a fresh look and feel to the movies. What these directors shared was a belief that truth was more important than slick production values. Hollywood was surprised to find that many of these films were popular in America even when they had subtitles. The next generations of American filmmakers would find their work inspiring.

ACTORS IN THE 50s

Rock Hudson and Doris Day were a good combination. They represented a world of charm and comfort, and their roles were traditional and reassuring. Neither was a rebel or threatened to rock the status quo. They were the kind of stars that always had a place in Hollywood. They were the kind of actors who could raise the level of the film and be entertaining just by their presence. The actors of the next generation would be quite different.

Doris Day

Doris Day was one of Hollywood's top box office performers through most of the 1950s and into the 1960s. She was originally a singer and often times sang in her movies. She had a lovely sweet hometown look that audiences liked. She was not voluptuously sexy like Marilyn Monroe but she was cute and smart without being threatening. She made three films with Rock Hudson. *Pillow Talk*, the first, set the mold.

Rock Hudson

Rock Hudson was the kind of actor that Hollywood appreciated. He was tall, handsome and charming. It took Hollywood a while to figure out the roles that suited Rock Hudson. Even though he was roughly John Wayne's size, he looked a little silly on a horse. Sometimes he was almost too handsome for the dramas that he was in. What he was good at was romantic comedy. Surprisingly, Rock Hudson turned down the script for *Pillow Talk* a number of times before finally accepting the role. He had not done light comedy before and was worried he would be ridiculous. It turned out romantic comedy is what he did best.

TRIVIA

Groucho Marx had one of the best lines about Doris Day. He said he knew her before she was a virgin, a reference to the fact that her screen roles were generally romantic but without any actual sex.

Rock Hudson was one of the first American celebrities to publicly announce that he was dying of AIDS and helped increase public awareness and sympathy for those afflicted by this new lethal disease.

Lover Come Back (1962), their last film together, is essentially the same film as *Pillow Talk*, just moved to the Madison Avenue the world of advertising.

Down With Love (2003) is the latest remake of *Pillow Talk*.

CHAPTER 17
1960s

The Graduate

Courtesy of Embassy/The Kobal Collection.

With astonishing speed, the Hollywood studio system that grew strong in the silent era, survived the Great Depression, thrived during WWII and stumbled during the '50s, finally collapsed in the '60s. For Hollywood, the 1960s would be a time of disintegration and then rebirth. It would be when the old way of making movies would die, and new stories would be told by new filmmakers in a new way for a new audience.

At the start of the '60s, Hollywood was in the doldrums, languishing under the weight of the Production Code, blacklisting and studio executives sadly out of touch with their audience. By 1970, Hollywood had reinvented itself. The Production Code was gone, replaced by the rating system. Blacklisting was over, irrelevant in an era of anti-war protesting and the realities of the Vietnam War. Finally, studio executives realized that there was a new audience for the movies, the baby boomers.

By 1970, box-office receipts, which had declined every year during the 1950s, now went up each year. The changes in Hollywood were fundamental and pervasive. A new kind of Hollywood emerged with the death of the Hollywood studio system.

DEATH OF THE PRODUCTION CODE

By the late 1960s, the Production Code that limited the kinds of stories that could be told was dead. It was replaced by the rating system which allowed for a much broader range of stories, graphic violence and nudity.

In 1965, *Who's Afraid of Virginia Woolf?* had censorship problems over words like bitch and bastard. In 1968 *Midnight Cowboy* had explicit homosexual encounters and full frontal nudity yet won an Academy Award for best picture. By the late '60s, the studios were not afraid of boycotts by moralistic pressure groups. The people who were threatening to boycott Hollywood movies were no longer Hollywood's audience. And the studios didn't own theaters, so they were much more difficult to target.

It also helped that during the '50s and '60s, rulings by the Supreme Court guaranteed freedom of expression in the movies. Graphic sexual imagery could no longer be banned automatically. What was most important for the studios was that there was a new audience for these sexually-adventuresome and graphic films.

BLACKLISTING FADES AWAY

By 1970, the blacklisting that had limited who could work and influenced the kind of stories that could be told was gone. By the mid '60s, McCarthyism and the Red Witch hunts of the '50s were not only gone but in disrepute.

To show how fast things changed, Dalton Trumbo, one of the Hollywood Ten, was blacklisted but used an assumed named to write an Academy Award-winning screenplay in 1956.

His Oscar for *The Brave One* was never picked up because the writer did not exist. Everybody knew who wrote the screenplay but had to pretend that this phantom writer was real. In 1960, Dalton Trumbo was one of the first blacklisted writers to get major studio screen credits, first for *Spartacus* and then for *Exodus*. In four short years, Dalton Trumbo went from invisible writer to celebrated artist. It did not happen all at once, but slowly during the '60s blacklisted writers found work.

THE HOLLYWOOD STUDIOS

Pity the studio executives of the early '60s. When they relied on standard formulas that worked so well in the past, the results were often mega flops.

Studio executives discovered that when they took risks with difficult, demanding material and gave newcomers a chance, they often succeeded.

Good examples were the films *Cleopatra* (1964) and *Who's Afraid of Virginia Woolf?* (1965). Both starred Elizabeth Taylor and Richard Burton. *Cleopatra* is an extravagant epic with a cast of thousands. The film went way over budget, almost bankrupted the studio and was a disaster at the box-office. *Who's Afraid of Virginia Woolf?* was shot in black-white by a young first-time director and a first-time cinematographer who shot much of the picture hand-held in a gritty documentary style. In the film, Elizabeth Taylor is fat, unglamorous and old. The gritty lighting emphasized the pock marks on Richard Burton's face. His character was a weak failure and the film had a downbeat ending.

This was not the kind of film Hollywood normally made. Yet, it won numerous Academy Awards and most importantly was a hit at the box-office. By the mid '60s, what movie audiences wanted had changed dramatically. Films of the '50s tended to be escapist and empty with feel-good moralistic happy endings.

The '50s ended with films like *Ben-Hur, The Nun's Story* and *Pillow Talk*, films with uplifting optimistic points of view. Contrast that with films from the late '60s such as *Bonnie and Clyde, The Wild Bunch* and *Easy Rider*, each with violent tragic endings. In these films the antiheroes died in a blaze of gunfire, yet the films were wildly popular.

In the '60s, audiences, particularly young audiences, wanted movies that were relevant to the major political and social upheavals that were convulsing the nation. The mid '60s were watershed years for the country, when the Vietnam War escalated, spawning huge draft calls and anti-war protests.

There were race riots in Watts, Newark, Detroit and Philadelphia that took tanks and the national guard to restore order. It was the time of the Haight Ashbury, LSD, sex, drugs and rock n' roll, of women's liberation and bra burnings. The leading edge of the baby boomers turned 18 in 1964. The baby boomers would be Hollywood's salvation, but their taste would be quite different from their parents'. It would take the studio executives a while to figure them out.

THE GRADUATE

The Graduate (1967) is one of those films that intuitively captured the heartbeat of the baby boomer generation. The film is not an explicit call for rebellion, and yet it is deeply seditious. The themes in the movie reflected the deep dissatisfaction that baby boomers had for the values of their parents and the world they were inheriting.

In 1967, America was torn apart by the Vietnam War. RFK and Martin Luther King were assassinated, and the threat of total nuclear war was real. It is not surprising that the baby boomers thought they could do better.

As Ben Braddock says in *The Graduate*, he wants his future to be "different." He is not sure what he wants, but he is sure he does not want to make the same choices his parents made. The swimming pools and fish tanks that are in so many scenes in *The Graduate* are important elements of the mise-en-scene. They are visual metaphors for the pampered but controlled life that awaits Ben. This is what Ben is rebelling against.

The Graduate shows how far film had gone in a short period of time. Just several years earlier the film could not have been made. The Production Code would not allow a story where a young man has an affair with an older married woman and then runs off with the woman's daughter. The rating system made these kinds of adult stories possible.

The very visuals of *The Graduate* are strikingly different from most films made by the studio system. The studio system emphasized uniformity and standardization.

Most films were shot and edited by a narrow set of rules. The Hollywood studios did not want to make arty, personal films. So, most studio films look very similar. The goal in most studio productions was to make the camera invisible.

Visually, *The Graduate* rebels against these stodgy, dated formulas. Much of the film is shot hand-held and there are numerous zooms and reveals that call attention to the camera work.

The editing is very different from the bland linear cutting in most studio films. In some scenes, the audio from the next scene precedes the visuals. For example, Ben calls Mrs. Robinson for their first meeting from the bottom of a swimming pool. Later, the scenes cutting back and forth between the hotel room, Mrs. Robinson, Ben and the swimming pool wonderfully convey Ben's state of mind. But they are well outside the standard storytelling techniques of most studio system films.

This was Mike Nichols' second film, his first was *Who's Afraid of Virginia Woolf?* and he was willing to take chances. Originally a comedian, he was a successful Broadway director before coming to Hollywood. The Broadway–Hollywood connection was a traditional path for studio system directors. In the '70s, a new path would emerge: film school.

Interestingly enough, the innovative camera work on *The Graduate* was done by Robert Surtees, an old time studio cinematographer who started in the '30s. Now for the first time, he was given the freedom to tell the story with an active camera.

In contrast to the visual freedom of *The Graduate*, Robert Surtees also shot *Ben-Hur*, a classic studio production where the camera work is invisible. For decades, the studio system stifled visual innovations; the late '60s would be a time of liberation.

The Graduate is Dustin Hoffman's first film. The studios originally wanted Robert Redford and Doris Day to play the lead roles. Anne Bancroft, who played Mrs. Robinson, was an Academy Award-winning actress but certainly not the box-office draw that Doris Day was.

It is interesting to note that when *The Graduate* was made, Anne Bancroft was 36 and played an older woman while Dustin Hoffman was 30 and played someone just turning 21. Some things in Hollywood never changed.

It is understandable that the studio would want a traditionally-handsome leading man like Robert Redford to play the lead in *The Graduate*. But Mike Nichols, the director, was adamant that Hoffman, an unknown Broadway actor, play the male lead. Even though Mike Nichols had only directed one movie before this, it was the highly-acclaimed and profitable *Who's Afraid of Virginia Woolf?* He was able to force the studio executives to use Hoffman.

Imagine the studio executives' chagrin when the three million dollar movie made more than $30 million at the box-office. This happened over and over in the late '60s and early '70s. Stories and actors that went against everything the studio executives had learned about making movies made money. Often, a lot of money.

Besides *The Graduate*, others like *Bonnie and Clyde*, *MASH*, *American Graffiti* and *Easy Rider* that ran counter to studio tastes were huge box-office hits. Hollywood Studio executives finally realized they did not have a clue about the kind of movies the baby boomers wanted to see. The solution was to bring in baby boomers to make films for baby boomers.

FRENCH NEW WAVE

The body of work by a new batch of French directors who came to prominence in the late '50s and early '60s was one of the strongest outside influences on American cinema of the late '60s. Lumped together by the term French New Wave, these directors shared numerous traits. Many had been film critics before becoming directors.

Most adored American films, particularly the films of Alfred Hitchcock. They loved the way Hitchcock was able to manipulate the emotions of an audience with camera and editing. The French New Wave directors had a disdain for the films of the French studio system with their large budgets and empty stories. Most were inspired by Italian directors sometimes called Neorealists of the late '40s who made films about ordinary people in ordinary situations.

These new directors wanted to make personal stories that reflected their vision. They were not concerned with box-office returns, stars and big budgets or attached to the perfection of a studio production. They wanted to capture truth by shooting from the heart. To do so, they were willing to violate normal editing and shooting conventions.

They were willing to shoot handheld and accept the jiggly images to run with the camera, to mix shooting styles, to mix humor with tragedy and to end films ambiguously. What was important to them was that their stories had meaning. Because their vision was personal, the films of the various French New Wave directors are quite different from each other.

The importance of the French New Wave films to Hollywood was that they brought a fresh filmic style and new kinds of stories to the screen. They showed Hollywood that there was a large audience for these kinds of films. Many of these films did well at the box-office, even though the New Wave films were in French with subtitles and confined to art house theaters.

By the early '70s, many of Hollywood's new directors, fresh out of film school, wanted to follow the lead of the French New Wave directors. They wanted to make films that meant something and they wanted to free the camera from being a passive recording instrument to an active part of the story telling process. *The Graduate* was simply one of the first films to use the innovations of the French Film New Wave in a Hollywood studio film. There were many, many more in the years to follow.

The combination of new filmic ideas from Europe, Japan and particularly France, the collapse of the old Hollywood studio system, the new baby boomer audience and the rise of a new breed of director all led to a rebirth of Hollywood in the '70s. The '70s was the generation of Lucas, Spielberg, Coppola and Scorsese. It led to personal films like *The Conversation*, *Taxi Driver* and *American Graffiti*.

Then surprisingly, it led to a new kind of film, the blockbuster. Films like *The Godfather*, *Jaws* and *Star Wars* transformed Hollywood in ways beyond anyone's wildest dreams. The '70s that began with unheard-of freedom for directors and writers, and so much promise, ended with corporate takeovers of the Hollywood studios and a new fixation on the bottom line.

CHAPTER 18

VIOLENCE 60s STYLE

Bonnie and Clyde

Courtesy of Warner Bros/The Kobal Collection.

Bonnie and Clyde is one of those films that leaps well beyond previous boundaries of filmmaking, dramatically changing the future direction of the movies. The mixture of a tender love story, verbal and slapstick comedy with graphic violence was difficult for many but struck exactly the right cord for the new audience for the movies—The Baby Boomers. The violence in *Bonnie and Clyde* is a quantum jump, more graphic and emotionally disturbing by far than anything made before. The violence is powerful and gut wrenching, but it is not gratuitous, sensational or misplaced.

Seeing a beautiful young woman ripped apart in slow motion by submachine gun fire is tough. It was supposed to be tough. And it was emotionally and narratively right. But it is not the bloodless violence that was an essential element of the Production Code and Hollywood film making for decades. Violence would now be a crucial part of Hollywood's future. This new emphasis on violence would be bloody and visually graphic if not necessarily realistic. But the violence would be emotionally effective and necessary to the underlying themes in many of the films of the period.

1960s

Graphic, powerful violence was part of the American world in the late '60s. Unlike today where much of the violence on television and in the news is random and personal, in the 1960s the violence was tied directly to political and social conflicts. On the nightly news were vivid imageries of body bags, firefights and the gruesome realities of the Vietnam War. In newspapers, magazines and television news, a running total was kept and updated continually of how many enemy, friendly and American soldiers were killed. Anything above 10 to 1 and we were winning. At the Democratic convention, the Chicago police rioted and beat demonstrators. In the summers, the National Guard in armored vehicles moved into riot-torn sections of Detroit, Newark,

Philadelphia and Watts now known as South Central Los Angeles. The bodies of three civil rights workers were recovered from an earthen dam in Mississippi. Two Kennedys were shot and killed. JFK's assassination was captured on film and replayed constantly on television. Bobby's last moments were captured in dramatic photographs. It was a violent time as society was torn and ripped by change. This violence was captured visually and shown to an eager mass audience.

The next generation—the baby boomers—would not be satisfied with the sugar-coated images that Hollywood produced in the '50s. Films in the late '60s would have to reflect the violent world they saw around them—not accurately like a documentary, but accurately emotionally. The visual violence on the screen would be a metaphor for the violence that seemed an integral part of the social and political changes that were happening to America.

NEW HEROES

The heroic but doomed outlaw would become the staple of late '60s filmmaking, often dying violently in a hail of bullets. Films, of course, had idealized outlaws before. But these were very different films in tone and attitude compared to the classic Hollywood gangster or western. In many westerns, outlaws and gun slingers became the heroes, forsaking their criminal ways to save a school marm, a child, a town, etc. Generally the gangster film, the criminal is a criminal because society has no place for his bravery, cunning and strength. Inevitably the gangster dies in the end because of his self-centered, selfish nature. He succeeds briefly only to be destroyed. The rules of society are proven not only virtuous but pragmatically correct.

In the history of Hollywood films, there have been many cynical heroes on the wrong side of the law, but always they chose to do the right thing in the end. Not Bonnie and Clyde. They never apologized for their actions or expressed a regret. When Bonnie asked Clyde what he would do differently, his answer amazed her. It is so child-like and naïve. His only regret is that he robbed banks in the same state he was living. He thought his problems would be over if they were in essence commuter bank robbers, robbing in one state and living peacefully in another. For the first time, the unrepentant criminal would become a common hero in Hollywood films. The outlaw of the '60s was an outlaw because society was wrong. The outlaws in late '60s films were not necessarily on the side of the angels, but at least they were not hypocrites.

BOX OFFICE TRENDS

As always, an important consideration for Hollywood is that *Bonnie & Clyde* made money, lots of money. In city after city, this lightly-regarded film had lines stretching down the block. Though many in the press and film critics in particular abhorred the violence and hated the film, a new young audience filled the theaters. The audience that Hollywood used to make movies for was gone, the baby boomers were now Hollywood's major audience. The old Hollywood made movies for everyone, now Hollywood would concentrate their attention on a core—the baby boomers.

For Hollywood, the crucial fact was that ticket sales were starting to rise. From the late '60s into the '90s, Hollywood would sell more tickets every year than the year before. Not close to what they sold in the '30s and '40s, but a lot more than during the 1950s. Graphic violence and rebellion against society would become standard story elements in the late '60s. For the next decade, Hollywood would make films that questioned America's history, future and dreams and make lots of money doing it. The trend wouldn't last; by the 1980s, the old Hollywood formulas would start to revive, but for a decade, new young directors would tell new stories with different themes and revitalize a tired Hollywood.

TRIVIA

After the film, berets—particularly for women—became a fashion trend for a short while.

C H A P T E R   19
1970s

The Godfather

Courtesy of Paramount/The Kobal Collection.

In Hollywood, the 1970s were a time of turmoil, freedom and rebirth. By 1980, the confusion was gone and so was much of the freedom. But for a short decade, Hollywood was open to new stories and new visions in a way that it had not been for a long, long time and would not be in the very near future.

The Godfather is classic Hollywood filmmaking but twisted and reshaped by new filmmakers with new attitudes. Perhaps this is what makes *The Godfather* so powerful—it artistically blends old formulas with new looks and sensibilities. The camera and editing are traditional linear Hollywood filmmaking, smooth and flawless. The story is epic in scope and scale in a way that suits Hollywood. It is a gangster version of *Gone with the Wind*—big and epic, yet personal as it focuses on family members in exceptional circumstances. This is the kind of story that Hollywood has always liked to make, full of suspense, drama, romance and intrigue. Nothing new here.

The innovations and changes from earlier eras of Hollywood filmmaking were subtle. The film is more real than normal for Hollywood. Not real or personal like European cinema, but with hints in that direction. There is little of the psychological nuances of French or English films of the period. But this is a family story, based at least loosely on real situations and real people. Several are sharp, canny and smart, but no one is superman or even particularly heroic. These are smart, dangerous individuals but within the realm of people we see in the newspapers everyday. But there is less glamour, less exaggeration, less suspension of disbelief in *The Godfather* than in most Hollywood films. Every character seems like a real person, in real situations with real motivations and real fears. This was not a revolutionary but a noticeable change as the studios adjusted to viewing taste of the early 1970s.

Visually what was most noticeable was that the film was much darker than most previous big budget Hollywood films. There is a long tradition of dark shadows and low light levels in many of the film noirs of the '40s or German films of the '20s and '30s, but with exceptions of course, Hollywood has always preferred a bright screen with bright, happy stories. The use of shadow and darkness as a visual metaphor in this film pushed the limits of traditional Hollywood filmmaking sensibilities, offended and disgusted studio executives while influencing numerous films to follow.

What Hollywood studio executives did notice was that this film made more money than any film since *Gone with the Wind*. Was it a fluke or was there something in this combination of old stories told in a visually-new way by the next generation of filmmakers that was artistically and financially powerful? On many levels, the answers were unsettling and deeply disturbing to traditional Hollywood studios.

THE GODFATHER

The Godfather was Hollywood's highest grossing film since *Gone with the Wind* 32 years earlier, and was part of a continuing trend that fundamentally reshaped the old Hollywood studio system into a new and improved Hollywood.

The Hollywood studio system did not usually try to make big-budget, high-grossing films. The studio system was designed to provide a steady stream of movies for a wide audience. They were looking for profits, of course, but not mega profit from one film. Consistent profit was the goal of studio system executives.

No one expected *The Godfather* to be a huge hit. The studio had acquired the film rights to *The Godfather* long before it was published and became a huge best seller. Literally a dozen directors were offered the script before Francis Ford Coppola. The studio was not anxious to make *The Godfather* because a big budget gangster film, *The Brotherhood*, starring Kirk Douglas had failed at the box-office the previous year and gangster pictures had not been popular since the early '30s.

Coppola was given *The Godfather* precisely because studio executives had little faith in the project. At the time, Coppola was a nobody in Hollywood terms. He had won an Academy Award as co-writer for *Patton*, and directed a couple of arty unremarkable films. There was no way studio executives would have trusted Coppola with *The Godfather* if they had any inkling of its blockbuster potential.

Coppola did not want to do the film. He said he only did it because he needed the money for the production company he and George Lucas were starting in San Francisco. He hated making the film and was almost fired a number of times during production.

Today, *The Godfather* seems to be a star-studded epic. But in 1972, Diane Keaton, Robert Duvall, James Caan and Al Pacino were all newcomers with no box-office appeal. Marlon Brando was a big star but was considered box-office poison and professionally unreliable. His last film, *Mutiny on the Bounty*, went way over budget because of Brando and then flopped at the box-office. The studio flatly refused to consider Brando for the role. In one meeting, the president of the studio told Coppola directly that Brando would never work for the studio. In the stuff of legends, Coppola was able to weasel, finagle, beg and lie his way into casting Brando and the newcomers over the strong objections of studio executives.

Once production began, the studio executives hated the way the film was shot. They hated that Brando mumbled his lines. They hated the lighting. Often you cannot see Brando's eyes. The whole film is dark and moody, particularly the interiors in the opening scene when the godfather is dispensing favors.

The studio executives wanted to fire the cinematographer. They wanted to fire Coppola. Instead, Coppola stayed, got what he wanted and the result was a mega-hit. Imagine the studio's chagrin. Studio executives resisted the casting, the story, the filmic look and repeatedly tried to fire the director of the highest-grossing film in 30 years.

In the early '70s, no one was quite sure what kinds of films were going to make money. So, in the uncertainty and confusion of the early '70s, there was tremendous opportunity for writers, producers and directors to get quirky personal projects made that would not have been considered in the Hollywood studio days. Many of the best films of the late '60s and early '70s, like *The Graduate, Bonnie and Clyde*, and *The Godfather* reflect this willingness to try something different. None of these are conventional Hollywood stories with traditional romances and feel good, happy endings. Yet each was hugely successful at the box-office.

It is easy to see the dilemma that these kinds of movies posed for studio executives. There is no common denominator between films like *The Graduate, Bonnie and Clyde*, and *The Godfather* except for a common sense of rebellion against traditional values, the fact that the young baby boomers loved them and they were made by Hollywood outsiders.

At first, *The Godfather* was seen as a fluke. Then came *Jaws*, then *Star Wars*. Blockbusters were no longer flukes. With this success, in a surprisingly short period of time, Hollywood moved from being wide open to new ideas and new people to a relatively closed system driven by profits and the bottom line. Within the decade, what emerged from the artistic freedoms of the early '70s was a restrictive narrow pattern of filmmaking as Hollywood became corporate.

Hollywood was forever transformed when these young outsiders became wildly successful. The amount of money *The Godfather* made altered the rules. At first, studio executives thought that the incredible success of *The Godfather* was just an odd combination of good luck. *The Godfather* (1972) was the first film to rock Hollywood with the scale of its success. *Star Wars* would push it off the cliff.

TRIVIA

A false horse's head was used during rehearsals but to add to the realism and the response of the actor for the actual shot, a real horse's head was used.

Paramount's original idea was to make this as a low-budget gangster film set in the present to save money rather than a period piece set in the 1940s and 1950s. They also wanted to shoot in Los Angeles instead of New York, again to save money.

It was the editor's idea to intercut the baptism scene with the gang killings.

James Caan broke two of Gianni Russo's ribs and chipped his elbow while pretending to beat his brother-in-law senseless.

C H A P T E R   20
CORPORATE HOLLYWOOD

Star Wars

Courtesy of Lucasfilm/20th Century Fox/The Kobal Collection.

*S*tar Wars fundamentally changed Hollywood forever. With films like *Jaws* and *The Godfather*, the Hollywood studios could sense that something had changed. These two films made huge amounts of money in a way that Hollywood was not used to and did not expect. They were both made by newcomers. *Jaws* is just Spielberg's second film, but neither *Jaws* nor *The Godfather* was a blueprint for future films. *The Godfather* and *Jaws* both were based on best-selling novels but have little else in common. Neither lends itself to a long series of sequels or as a blueprint to a new formula for making films. There would be sequels to both and *The Godfather Part II* would be a huge commercial and artistic success. But neither is the kind of film that can be duplicated in a more general way.

Star Wars, on the other hand, is exactly what Hollywood can do and has been doing from the beginning. *Star Wars* is, to borrow a line describing *Casablanca*, "sophisticated hokum." *Star Wars* can be done over and over again: idealistic youth, jaded veteran, the evil empire, beautiful princess, romance, suspense, danger, can all be mixed in various combinations in all kinds of stories, in all kinds of places, and all kinds of eras.

The reliance on visual special effects is also something that suits the Hollywood studios. Special effects need a tremendous amount of planning and control. So, in some sense, a film that relies on substantial special effects is almost pre shot. The director is not as important in a special effects-heavy film. In Hollywood terms, the film is not execution dependent. That is, it does not need great acting, spectacular cinematography, nuanced directing or riveting editing. A solid adventure story and spectacular visual effects are enough.

Star Wars is a visual and emotional treat. As has been said many times, *Star Wars* is a visual amusement park in a tried and true format. The ending is happy, evil is conquered, justice triumphs, the jaded are reborn, romance is in the air. Hollywood has been making these kinds of films since the turn of the 20th century.

It is not by accident that many people have seen the similarities between *Casablanca* and *Star Wars*. The elements are essentially the same. Lucas simply mixed a classic Hollywood love story with the scale and the epic scope of Kurosawa's *Hidden Fortress*, morphing the two into something unique, and yet something that could be duplicated.

Now Hollywood could see what kind of films to make. No need to trust their fate and careers to young nobodies or oddball ideas. Quickly the goal of the Hollywood studio became to make fewer and fewer films with bigger and bigger budgets that rely on visual effects and exciting stories to attract a young mass audience.

THE INDEPENDENTS

One of the odd results of Hollywood becoming focused on making big-budget block-busters was that small independent film flourished. Since Hollywood was producing fewer films, there were more opportunities to have an independent film reach the theater since the advent of the Cineplex meant there were a lot of screens available. At the same time, the studios realized that they could make money on independent films. Let the independents find the stories, write the scripts, finance the films, then the studios would distribute them for a healthy cut of the box office. After all, who better than the studios knew how to market films. What independent producer or director wanted to spend his time, money and energy figuring out how to show the film in Manila, Hong Kong, Rome, London, Topeka or Atlanta and keep track of all the expenses, currency conversion, import/export licenses, etc? This was what the studios did everyday. Let the independents take the risks. The studios would make the profits.

So quickly, a two-tiered system developed. Big budget films like *ET*, *Raiders of the Lost Ark*, *Lord of the Rings*, etc are made by studios. Smaller budget films like *Room with a View*, *Fargo*, and *My Big Fat Greek Wedding* are produced independently and then distributed by a major studio. The independent keeps control of projects that are personally meaningful and the studios make money, lots of money. Each year starting in the late '60s into the 1990s, box office receipts go up every year—not to the levels of the 1940s but with a much brighter future than the 1950s.

CORPORATE HOLLYWOOD

Precisely because of the box office success of films like *The Graduate*, *Bonnie and Clyde*, then *The Godfather* and *Star Wars*, the traditional Hollywood studios became attractive takeover targets for non-filmmaking corporations. The irony is that Hollywood became corporate because the renegade, rebellious directors, writers and producers of the early '70s were so successful that outside corporations decided that it made perfect financial sense to own a Hollywood studio.

Many of the original Hollywood studios began as family businesses and stayed that way until the death or retirement of the original founders. Warner Brothers, started in the 1920s, was owned and operated by the four Warner brothers well into the 1950s. Columbia also began in the 1920s and was run by Jack and Harry Cohn, from the beginning until the mid 50s. Walt Disney, of course, founded Disney and ran it until his death in 1966.

Today, Warner Brothers is a relatively small piece of AOL Time Warner, a huge global media company that owns magazine, music, Internet and movie businesses. Coca Cola bought Columbia in 1982. Today Columbia is owned by Sony. General Electric owns NBC and Universal Studios. Disney is owned by Capitol, a media conglomerate that also owns the American Broadcasting Company television network.

The corporatization of Hollywood that began to gather steam in the '60s intensified during the '70s, '80s and '90s. As an additional irony, the initial freedom that directors and producers had at the beginning of the '70s was mostly gone by the start of the 1980s. Studio executives now had clear ideas of what kinds of films they wanted to make. A few big-budget special effects action pictures, a few youth-oriented films and maybe a romantic comedy or two—that was the way to make money in the new improved Hollywood. The old Hollywood studio system was now dead but there was a new system that took its place. The rules were different but in many ways just as rigid.

Not only were there new owners and new rules for the studios, but the basic business relationships between the talent side of the business—actors, writers, directors and producers—and studio executives changed dramatically in the 1960s.

In the studio system, everyone had long-term contracts at one studio and made the kind of films the studio executives wanted to make. By the '60s, in a slow and evolutionary process, most talent worked from picture to picture. There were no long-term contracts and everyone was free to move from studio to studio, film to film as projects became available.

TRIVIA

The MPAA originally rated *Star Wars* G, but studio execs had it changed to PG before release because teenagers might consider it a "kids' movie."

At one point, Lucas had planned the character of Han Solo to be a huge green-skinned monster with no nose and gills; later he considered making Han Solo black.

Studio executives were unhappy that Chewbacca had no clothes and attempted to have him wear shorts.

20th Century Fox thought that the major audience for *Star Wars* was teenage comic-book-reading males.

Fewer than 40 theaters agreed to show *Star Wars* when first offered the opportunity.

Luke started out as a woman, then he was a dwarf, then a 60 year-old general. His name was changed from Luke Starkiller to Luke Skywalker on the first day of shooting.

Universal and United Artists both turned down a chance to make *Star Wars*.

20th Century Fox was so sure *Star Wars* was going to be a disaster that they came within a matter of days of selling off their stake in the film as a tax shelter. Positive feedback from an advanced screening made them change their minds.

Within three weeks of the film's release, 20th Century Fox's stock price doubled to a record high, saving them from the verge of bankruptcy.

To entice a reluctant studio into making the film, Lucas agreed to forgo his directing salary in exchange for 40 percent of the film's box-office take and all merchandising rights.

Within a year of its release *Star Wars* had taken in more than $200 million at the box office and millions of dollars in toys and merchandise. The studios would not make that kind of mistake again.

C H A P T E R   21

FILM SCHOOL

Boyz N the Hood

Courtesy of Columbia/The Kobal Collection.

By the mid 1980s striking, substantial change came to Hollywood, altering the kinds of films that were made, as well as who got to make movies. Finally women and minorities started to have a voice in Hollywood. It was not a loud voice and it was not equal. But it started for women and minorities about the same time and for the same reason—film schools. Film schools changed the dynamics and the possibilities. But the results were uneven, as some minorities did much better than others. Ultimately, women, African Americans, Asians and Hispanics all had different results as Hollywood changed in the 1980s. The reasons are specific to each group. But the opportunities came in general because of the advent of film school.

Almost from the beginning, Hollywood had been a white male-dominated business. There were almost no minorities in the beginning, but early on there had been a number of women directing and producing short films, mostly comedies. But with the coming of features, big budgets, big business, and the studio system, women had been relegated to a number of important but limited roles, mostly as actors, screen writers, or editors.

Generation after generation, there were very, very few minorities in Hollywood. There were usually just a few in front of the camera, almost none behind the camera, in the crafts, or in the executive offices. Generally, for most of Hollywood's history, there were no minorities or women producing or directing. That changed relatively quickly in the mid 1980s—but not because Hollywood finally saw the error of its ways or suddenly became politically correct. What happened was Hollywood just being Hollywood.

MINORITIES/WOMEN IN HOLLYWOOD

By the mid 1980s women and minorities coming out of film school began to have an impact on Hollywood. Directors like Amy Heckerling, Spike Lee, and Wayne Wang showed Hollywood that women and minority directors could make films that made money. Hollywood also learned that films with minority characters, telling minority stories, could find an audience and make money. By the late 1980s, it was clear that with the right story, white audiences would turn out for certain kinds of stories even if the cast was predominately African American. For generations, Hollywood had been afraid that films with mostly African American actors telling black stories would not do well in many parts of the country. What Spike Lee and others showed was that times had changed. There was not a market for every minority and every story, but under the right circumstances and with the right characters, there were significant profits to be made. These insights came from the success of films made outside of the Hollywood Studios. Most films with minority or women directors were independently financed with substantially smaller budgets than the Hollywood norm, and most of these independent films were made by filmmakers fresh out of film school.

FILM SCHOOL

University programs that concentrate on developing new film makers are a relatively recent occurrence. Most film schools started in the 1960s. They usually expanded from an academic look at the history, meaning and art of film into becoming almost trade schools, teaching students the nuts, bolts, and business of filmmaking. There were not only courses in screenwriting and film production, but producing, marketing, contracts, distribution, etc. Many of the instructors were former or current Hollywood filmmakers. Some of the best universities in the country quickly developed major film programs. For decades now, USC, UCLA, and NYU have been three of the top film programs in the country.

The first generation of film school graduates were people like Francis Ford Coppola (UCLA). Then a few years later came directors like George Lucas (USC) and Martin Scorsese (NYU). These directors and others like them came out of film school and changed Hollywood. The second generation of directors and screenwriters that came out of film school also changed Hollywood in fundamental ways, if not in quite as spectacular fashion.

Film schools not only gave women and minorities a chance to learn the craft and make films, but just as importantly the chance to make connections with other talented filmmakers. Hollywood is now full of people who met in film school, worked on each other's projects, appreciated each other's abilities and complemented each other's talents. Now they are creative teams. One might be a writer/director, the other a producer. Some cinematographers work over and over with the same director. A writer might find a symbiotic relationship with a producer/director. Whatever the skill set, creative teams have an advantage in bringing films to the screen, since it is hard for one person to be great at everything. Hollywood has long had many successful creative teams. The difference is that individuals today are first coming together in film school.

One big advantage that film schools provide is that they give students with the drive, talent, and perseverance the opportunity to get a first feature made. If that first feature is a hit—and it is a big if—Hollywood is willing to listen. No guarantees, but the door is at least ajar. This is a new pathway. This is one of the reasons that it is possible to be an independent filmmaker today and to go from micro budgets to mega budgets in just a few films. Before 1960, it was very, very difficult to make films independently. Between 1920 and 1950, it was almost impossible.

WOMEN

In the early 1950s, out of roughly 1,400 members of the Directors Guild, only two were women. Of those two, one was retired, and the other made films independently. Today, roughly 20 percent of the Directors Guild are women. Women became more prominent as producers during the 1970s and as directors during the 1980s. Many made their first films independently after graduating from film schools. In recent years, several studio heads have been women. Still, women directors in Hollywood face significant ongoing obstacles.

Roughly half of the features films made today are written and directed by the same person. There is a maxim in Hollywood to write what you know—to make films that you personally want to see, that you have a passion for, that touch you or move you in some personal way. It is not required but it is a useful generality. As a generality—and there are notable exceptions—women tend to be more interested in stories that involve emotional discoveries and emotional adventures versus car chases, explosions, and epic adventures. For better or worse, top box office films these days tend to be action adventure, special effects-laden, male-dominated extravaganzas which do well worldwide. Today, overseas box office potential is a crucial factor in the studio movie-making decision process. Films with women as the leading characters tend to be smaller in scale, more emotional in tone and though they may do well in the US, tend not to do nearly as well overseas. So though there are lots of women in Hollywood directing and in the executive office, it is certainly not a 50-50 world.

MINORITIES

Since the mantra in most college film writing courses is to write what you know and to make films that you are passionate about, it is no surprise that most minority directors' first films were stories where minorities were the central characters. What surprised Hollywood was not just that film schools were producing very talented people but that minority stories did very well at the box office. Generally, Hollywood is reluctant to change without knowing the changes will make money. It is not that telling minority stories suddenly became trendy or easy, but once it became clear that some minority stories were making money, Hollywood began to pay attention. But not all minority stories are created equally. Hollywood was quick to realize that certain minorities were better box office than others. Some of this is just simple demographics. African Americans make up roughly 13 percent of the population and buy perhaps 20 percent of the box office tickets. That is significant size. Asians as a group are less that five percent of the US population and their impact on box office performance has been relatively minimal.

Women, of course, are roughly half the population and by many estimates account for 60 percent of the box office buying decisions, but that size has not translated into box office punch. Ultimately Hollywood does not care who makes movies or what stories get told, but it does care deeply and fundamentally about whether the films make money. The box office decides. This has been true for American filmmaking since the beginning and it is no less true today.

BOYZ N THE HOOD

Boyz n the Hood is a good illustration of studio thinking at the beginning of the 1990s. Early Spike Lee films had demonstrated that there was a significant audience for stories featuring African American casts. It was also clear that the racial climate in this country had changed to the point that a generally-white audience was willing to pay to see interesting stories with mostly African American characters. The cast and story arc of *Boyz n the Hood* would have been unthinkable 10 years earlier but was common by the early 1990s. The change in stories and directors starting in the mid 1980s meant that many new actors had opportunities that did not exist before. The opportunities were not equal for all minorities and certainly it is still not easy to tell stories based on minority experiences, but particularly for African American male actors, there were options that did not exist before.

JOHN SINGLETON

John Singleton, the director and writer of *Boyz n the Hood*, went to University of Southern California Film School. He had won a number of screenwriting awards and the studio was comfortable with financing and supporting his first film. It would have been unimaginable just a few years before to finance an untried filmmaker, let alone a film with mostly African American actors. But Spike Lee and others' success convinced a major studio that this was a worthwhile project that could make money. With studio funding and support, the budget was significantly larger than most first features. The studio did exercise a significant amount of control to make sure that the film was of commercial quality. But ultimately what was most important was that the film was both a creative and financial success. The continued success of films with mostly African American characters meant that Hollywood would at least be willing to listen.

The themes in *Boyz n the Hood* were also strikingly effective. John Singleton not only showed the audience what the roots of the violence were and the problems the violence caused, but he offered a solution. It was a solution that required nothing more than men to be good fathers. The situations explored in *Boyz n the Hood* have not gone away. From Miami to Oakland, the Bronx to South Central, young black males still kill each other at an alarming rate for often trivial reason. Hollywood, though, has moved on and so have the opportunities for African American directors and actors. The changes are certainly not complete or particularly pervasive and deep, but it has allowed for African American directors to also work in genres outside of inner urban youth films.

AFRICAN AMERICAN

It is not easy to be an actor in general. And there is nothing fair about the way Hollywood goes about casting movies. Hollywood is definitely not an equal opportunity employer. But it is easy to see that the range of stories and characters available for African American males has changed dramatically since the 1980s. It has reached the point where big budget films can be carried by an African American lead. This does not mean that Hollywood is interested in just any minority story, but it does mean that it is not automatically rejected. The changes for African American women are not nearly so dramatic, but this reflects Hollywood's lack of interest in female leads more than any concern about ethnicity. Simply put, Hollywood has decided big budget, special-effects driven action pictures do not necessarily need big name actors but the lead is almost always male.

ASIAN

Even to the casual observer it is easy to see that there are very few Asian actors on the screen. The few that exist tended to be stars in Hong Kong first. Again, there are few opportunities for Asian women in major roles in Hollywood movies. A number of Asian directors have done well in Hollywood. Wayne Wang and Ang Lee both went to film school in the US and have made a number of films here and in Asia. Other directors like John Woo started in Asia and are now directing Hollywood movies. But they are the exception. There are also a few Asian women directors, but again just a few.

LATINO/LATINA

Because the Latino population in this country is growing so quickly and is now the largest minority group in America, one would think that there would start to be a number of Latino actors and stories coming out of Hollywood. So far that has not been the case. The television, radio, cable and broadcast areas have grown exponentially in the last few years but so far Hollywood, with a few exceptions of course, has not responded to this potential. It may be because the Latino population is so diverse, coming from so many countries and so many cultures that make them unique, that it is hard for Hollywood to distill that experience into a film that would appeal to such a broad population.

TODAY

Today roughly 75 percent of the writers, directors, and producers in Hollywood are white males. The percentages are even higher among the editors and cinematographers. And the number of minority actors that are considered bankable are few. But 75 percent is a long way from the 99 percent of just several decades ago. It is certainly not equal but the door is not locked and the key has been Film School.

TRIVIA

Ice Cube was John Singleton's first choice for Doughboy.

Many of the characters in the film were based on people John Singleton knew growing up.

At 24, John Singleton was the youngest director ever nominated for an Oscar.

As a return on investment, *Boyz n the Hood* was 1991's most financially successful film, making $56.1 million on a budget of $6.5 million.

Laurence Fishburne, who plays Cuba Gooding Jr.'s father, is only six and a half years older than him in real life.

HOLLYWOOD TODAY

Crash

Courtesy of Lions Gate/The Kobal Collection.

Today there are basically two ways that films are financed. They are either produced by one of the major Hollywood studios or they are independently produced. Major Hollywood studio films generally have one of two characteristics, either they have big stars and a big budget or a mega budget with incredible special effects. The budgets for independently-produced films are much smaller, but there may be well-known actors, and even big-time stars. The budget range for independent films can be almost nothing up to $20 million or more, and recently a few independent films have approached $60 million. In contrast, a number of recent Hollywood studio productions have had budgets well over $200 million and seem likely to top $300 million in the near future.

But, there is much more than budgets, special effects and dollars that separate independent and Hollywood studio films. Independent films tend to be about something. At the core of independent films there are usually fundamental human dilemmas. Though every film, no matter the budget size, must have conflicts and drama to be successful, independent films tend to focus around moral dilemmas that often have no easy or reassuring answer. Major blockbuster films from *Batman* and *Superman* to *Spiderman*, *Lord of the Rings*, and *King Kong* tend to focus more on the physical jeopardy of likable characters than on any underlying moral dilemmas the characters face. The dilemmas that superheroes tend to face are personal and not a question of basic human values.

There are many reasons that the Hollywood studios prefer big budget films: big-budget films like *Batman* and *Spiderman* often lend themselves to sequels. This means the studios are guaranteed strong box office results for years. Small independent films rarely have any potential to be sequels, which means even if it is a hit; the studio must literally go back to a blank piece of paper to start all over again looking for the next sleeper hit. It is no way to run a studio; it is a guaranteed way to go broke in a hurry. It is difficult enough to make a few big-budget movies that make money without having to continually find numerous, creative, artistic projects that can find an audience.

In Hollywood terms, independent films are execution dependent, that is, the director and actors must create a memorable film out of the script writer's words and intensions. Special effects-dominated movies, though much more expensive, are by the very nature of the process much easier to evaluate and control. Special effects take months and months of planning, sketching, drawing, and artwork before they ever become film. This necessarily-painstaking approach to special effects means there is continual opportunity to evaluate sequences for their cinemagraphic potential. This kind of oversight provides much more control and much more of a guarantee of box office success than simply gambling on whether an actor is right for the part and the director can capture that elusive quality that generates audience interest.

It may seem like a contradiction, but for the Hollywood studios, a $200 million epic extravaganza is much less risky than any $20 million film. And there is, of course, much more upside potential. There is just way too much that can go wrong and way too much that has to go right in a medium-budget film to make money. Certainly, the chances of making money with ten $20 million films are much less than with one $200 million film and a lot less grief, worry and effort. The Hollywood studios would much rather risk their box office fortunes for the year on one or two mega-budget films than try to make a number of modest- to medium-budget films.

For Hollywood, trying to make a large number of medium-budget, quality, entertaining films is a sure recipe for going broke. The Hollywood studios will let the independents scurry around to raise money from whatever sources to make more personal, character-driven films. For Hollywood, small films that tell small stories with small budgets have almost no potential to change the bottom line of a major studio. Even if they are successful and make money, it will not be anywhere large enough to change the financial fortunes of a Hollywood studio.

Just as importantly, Hollywood does not see the independent filmmakers as competitors. Just the opposite. The Hollywood studios are quite willing to let independents take all the risks—write the script, raise the money, cast and shoot the film and when they are done, the Hollywood studios will compete for the opportunity to distribute the film. The money in all filmmaking is in distribution. Making a film just costs money. Distributing a film is when the money comes back. If someone else has put up all the money to make the film there is very little risk in distributing the film. It is very difficult to look at a script and decide whether it is worth investing $5 million, $20 million, or $50 million. It is much, much easier to gauge whether or not a story has box office potential once the film is completed.

So, once a film is done, the studios are happy to step in and try to make money on smaller films. And the independents need the studios. After all, distributing films is what the studios do best. The Hollywood studios know their demographics and their markets. They know how to develop an advertising campaign. They know in which theaters in Boston, Omaha and Phoenix to play which films. And just as importantly, they know in which theaters in Berlin, Manila and Tokyo to show which kinds of American films. They know how to convert Euros, pesos, and yen into dollars. Few filmmakers want the headaches and the bother of distributing their own films. Besides, most independents do not have the expertise or the capital. A release print for a two hour film will cost roughly two thousand dollars. To release that film on five hundred screens will cost a million dollars. Advertising and publicity will cost millions more. Most independents do not have the money or the energy once the movie is done. So Hollywood today is a two-tiered system. Hollywood makes big-budget films and distributes the rest.

FILM FESTIVALS

Film festivals have proliferated in the last decade as a means for independents to show their films to audiences. It is not difficult to sit in the back of a theater and gauge an audience's reaction to a film. Once the film is made, it is no longer guesswork. Then it becomes just marketing and selling. That is much, much simpler than betting millions of dollars on black ink on white paper. So filmmakers who want control of their films or who have stories to tell that are personal will need to raise the money outside of Hollywood. If they are successful, and the film has the potential to find an audience, then Hollywood major studios are willing to distribute and promote.

So it is not by accident that in the last few years, the most critically acclaimed, the most award-winning and nominated films have been made outside of the Hollywood studios. At the same time, the top box office films generating oodles and oodles of cash have been studio projects. Films like *Lord of the Rings*, and the Harry Porter series have literally produced billions of dollars in worldwide ticket sales. So today, film awards tend to be dominated by independent films and the box office dominated by Hollywood blockbusters.

CRASH

Crash is not a particularly great film nor will it change Hollywood filmmaking, but it is a good example of these independently-produced films. It had an established director, writer, and a number of well-known actors in the ensemble cast. It had a budget of roughly $6 million, when the Hollywood average is closer to $50 million. There was money to be made even though it did not do particularly well in the box office, especially for an Academy Award-winning film. But with $50 million at the box office and a $6 million film budget, there were significant profits. Of course *Crash* produced tens of millions of dollars, not the hundreds of millions of dollars that is the goal of most Hollywood studios. None of the films nominated for best picture in 2006 were big box office films. They were quirky, critically acclaimed, stimulating but not tempting for a mass audience. They were films about race relations, alienation, a gay cowboy love story, a gay writers' dilemma, a TV journalist's moral dilemma and a thoughtful look at the moral implications of a war on terrorism. In fact, all the 2006 nominees had at their core a look at the moral predicaments the characters faced.

Hollywood is not about posing or solving moral dilemmas, it is about making money. So it is not a surprise that films that centered around moral dilemmas would be critically acclaimed but likely lag at the box office. And it should not be surprising that none of the best picture Academy Award nominees for 2005 were in the top 20 for box office performance. *Crash*, the winner, was 49th. If Hollywood is about making money, then the studio executives were right: they made films that made money, and distributed the films that won awards. Of course they also make money distributing and that's how Hollywood works today.

TRIVIA

Paul Haggis the director was carjacked a few years before making *Crash*.

With a budget of $6 million for this film, director Paul Haggis cut costs by using his own house for scenes and even his own car for other scenes.

The script was written in 2001. This is a common lag time in most films. It always takes awhile to either raise the money or get studio backing.

Lions Gate bought the distribution rights to the film for $4 million at the 2004 Toronto International Film Festival.

First film bought in a film festival (Toronto) to win an Academy Award for best picture.

Surprisingly this is the first movie to be set primarily in Los Angeles and win a Best Picture Oscar.

AFTERWARDS

Hollywood today is in a state of flux. Of course Hollywood is and always has been in a state of flux. From decade to decade, Hollywood has changed and evolved. Every decade has been fundamentally different with different genres, different directors, different stars, different looks and stories. What has not changed in Hollywood is that box office is king and determines Hollywood's next evolution. This was Hollywood from the beginning. Almost from film to film, Hollywood adapts and changes. The success of a film leads to many imitations. Box office failure leads to a dead end and Hollywood tries again. In some sense, every film is an experiment, a question mark that only the box office and the audience can answer.

Hollywood faces many vexing questions today; viewership and box office takes are shrinking. There is the threat and reality of piracy and the Internet. Budgets for blockbuster films have skyrocketed. Budgets over $200 million are becoming commonplace. Young audiences seem uninterested and unmoved by the movies. But human beings like to tell stories, like to listen to stories, and that hasn't changed. I have no idea what Hollywood will look like in 10 years, or even five years. I am sure that it will be different because that has been Hollywood's story from the beginning.

But what I am sure of is that as long as Hollywood makes films that touch us emotionally, that make us laugh, that enlighten us, that encourage us, then Hollywood will have a significant place in our culture and our lives. The stories may change, the financing may change, who tells the stories may change, the technology may change, and it is clear the stories will change, but people's need for stories will not go away. And as long as people want entertaining stories that touch their hearts and lives, then there will be a place for Hollywood films.

The following films were chosen because they capture the flavor of an era, a genre or a director. Many great films are not included and not every included film is great. But they are worth watching. At least in my opinion. Enjoy.

RECOMMENDED FILMS

FILM 1900–1910
Life of an American Fireman (1903)
The Policemen's Little Run (1907)
The Whole Dam Family and the
　Dam Dog (1905)
The Mermaid (1904)
The Living Playing Cards (1904)
The Black Imp (1905)
The Enchanted Sedan Chair (1905)

D. W. GRIFFITH
Intolerance (1916)
Broken Blossoms (1919)
Way Down East (1920)
Orphans of the Storm (1922)
The Lonedale Operator (1911)
The Musketeers of Pig Alley (1912)

CHARLIE CHAPLIN
The Pawn Shop (1916)
The Rink (1916)
The Immigrant (1917)
The Kid (1921)
The Gold Rush (1925)
The Circus (1928)
Modern Times (1936)
The Great Dictator (1940)

SILENT FILM 1910–1927
Quo Vadis (1912)
The Squaw Man (1914)
The Virginian (1914)
The Mark of Zorro (1920)
High and Dizzy (1920)
Tillie's Punctured Romance (1914)
The Ten Commandments (1923)
The General (1924)
Cops (1922)

The Camera Man (1928)
Safety Last (1923)
Never Weaken (1921)
The Freshman (1925)
The Married Widow (1925)
Metropolis (1927)
Nosferatu (1922)
Sun Rise (1927)
The Last Laugh (1924)
The Big Parade (1925)
The Jazz Singer (1927)

THE COMING OF SOUND / *SCARFACE*
Underworld (1936)
The Public Enemy (1931)
All Quiet on the Western Front
　(1930)
I Am a Fugitive from a Chain Gang
　(1932)
Little Caesar (1931)
The Dawn Patrol (1938)

**PRECODE FILMS / *RED DUST* AND
*TROUBLE IN PARADISE***
Morocco (1930)
The Blue Angel (1930)
Blond Venus (1932)
Shanghai Express (1932)
She Done Him Wrong (1933)
I'm No Angel (1933)
Baby Face (1933)

**SCREWBALL COMEDY /
*IT HAPPENED ONE NIGHT***
Mr. Deeds Goes to Town (1936)
Mr. Smith Goes to Washington
　(1939)
The Awful Truth (1937)

Bringing Up Baby (1938)
His Girl Friday (1940)
Ball of Fire (1941)
The Philadelphia Story (1940)
Adam's Rib (1949)

RECENT VERSIONS
Sweet Home Alabama (2002)
Maid In New York (2002)
Two Weeks Notice (2002)
When Harry Met Sally (1989)
What's Up Doc? (1972)
Overboard (1987)
50 First Dates (2004)

WESTERNS / *STAGECOACH*
My Darling Clementine (1946)
The Searchers (1956)
The Man Who Shot Liberty Valance
   (1962)
Red River (1948)
Rio Bravo (1959)
Rio Lobo (1970)
The Outlaw (1943)
High Noon (1952)
Shane (1953)
Johnny Guitar (1954)
The Magnificent Seven (1960)
The Wild Bunch (1969)
McCabe and Mrs. Miller (1971)
High Plains Drifter (1972)
The Good, the Bad and the Ugly (1966)
For a Few Dollars More (1965)
The Shootist (1976)
Pale Rider (1985)
Dances with Wolves (1990)
Unforgiven (1992)
Destry Rides Again (1939)
Blazing Saddles (1974)
The Wild Bunch (1969)

Pat Garrett and Billy the Kid (1973)
High Plains Drifter (1973)
True Grit (1969)
Butch Cassidy and the Sundance Kid
   (1969)

HOLLYWOOD REBEL / *CITIZEN KANE*
The Magnificent Ambersons (1942)
The Lady from Shanghai (1947)
Touch of Evil (1958)
The Third Man (1949)

THE STUDIO SYSTEM / *CASABLANCA*
Gunga Din (1939)
The Pride of the Yankees (1942)
The Grapes of Wrath (1940)
Grand Hotel (1932)
Captain Blood (1935)
The Sea Hawk (1940)
Yankee Doodle Dandy (1942)
Dark Victory (1939)
The Adventures of Robin Hood
   (1938)
Gone with the Wind (1939)
The Wizard of Oz (1939)
The Best Years of Our Lives (1946)
The Treasure of the Sierra Madre
   (1948)

*CASABLANCA REMAKES AND
KNOCKOFFS*
To Have and Have Not (1944)
Havana (1990)

GENRE / *THE PALM BEACH STORY*
The Great McGinty (1940)
The Lady Eve (1941)
Sullivan's Travels (1941)
The Miracle of Morgan's Creek
   (1944)

FILM NOIR
The Maltese Falcon (1941)
Murder, My Sweet (1944)
Detour (1945)
Mildred Pierce (1945)
Scarlette Street (1945)
The Killers (1946)
Crossfire (1947)
Out of the Past (1947)
The Lady from Shanghai (1948)
The Naked City (1948)
Gun Crazy (1949)
DOA (1950)
Touch of Evil (1958)
The Big Sleep (1946)

NEO NOIR
Body Heat (1981)
The Last Seduction (1994)
Chinatown (1974)
The Big Sleep (1978)
L.A. Confidential (1997)
Blood Simple (1984)
The Grifters (1990)
Devil in a Blue Dress (1995)

BLACKLISTING / *THE FRONT*
The Weavers: Wasn't That a Time (1982)
Good Night, and Good Luck (2005)
Guilty by Suspicion (1991)

THE 1950s / *ON THE WATERFRONT*
Gentlemen's Agreement (1947)
A Streetcar Named Desire (1951)
Viva Zapata! (1952)
Singin' in the Rain (1952)
Stalag 17 (1953)
From Here to Eternity (1953)
The Wild One (1953)
East of Eden (1955)
12 Angry Men (1957)
A Face in the Crowd (1957)

CLASSICAL HOLLYWOOD STYLE / *REAR WINDOW*
The Man Who Knew Too Much (1934)
The 39 Steps (1935)
Rebecca (1940)
Shadow of a Doubt (1943)
Lifeboat (1944)
Rope (1948)
Strangers on a Train (1951)
Dial M for Murder (1954)
To Catch a Thief (1955)
The Trouble with Harry (1955)
The Man Who Knew Too Much (1956)
Vertigo (1958)
North by Northwest (1959)
Psycho (1960)
The Birds (1963)

SEX 1950s STYLE / *PILLOW TALK*
Lover Come Back (1962)
The Touch of Mink (1963)
Giant (1956)
Some Like It Hot (1959)
The Seven Year Itch (1955)
How to Marry a Millionaire (1953)
Gentlemen Prefer Blondes (1953)

1960s / *THE GRADUATE*
Pretty in Pink (1986)
The Breakfast Club (1985)
Diner (1982)
Harold and Maude (1971)

Sixteen Candles (1984)

Ferris Bueller's Day Off (1986)

Risky Business (1983)

American Pie (1999)

Stand by Me (1986)

My Life as a Dog (1985)

The Cider House Rules (1999)

400 Blows (1959)

Rebel Without a Cause (1955)

Saturday Night Fever (1977)

Fast Times at Ridgemont High
(1982)

Good Will Hunting (1998)

VIOLENCE 60s STYLE / *BONNIE AND CLYDE*

The Wild Bunch (1969)

Straw Dogs (1971)

Taxi Driver (1976)

Badlands (1973)

A Clockwork Orange (1971)

Cool Hand Luke (1967)

Easy Rider (1969)

Midnight Cowboy (1969)

Dirty Harry (1971)

In Cold Blood (1967)

The Texas Chainsaw Massacre (1974)

1970s / *THE GODFATHER*

The Brotherhood (1968)

The Conversation (1974)

The Godfather Part II (1974)

The Godfather Part III (1990)

The Cotton Club (1984)

Rumble Fish (1983)

Apocalypse Now (1979)

Jaws (1975)

Annie Hall (1977)

MASH (1970)

CORPORATE HOLLYWOOD / *STAR WARS*

Close Encounters of the Third Kind
(1977)

Raiders of the Lost Ark (1981)

E.T. the Extra-Terrestrial (1982)

Indiana Jones and the Temple of
Doom (1984)

Indiana Jones and the Last Crusade
(1989)

Jurassic Park (1993)

The Empire Strikes Back (1980)

The Phantom Menace (1999)

The Terminator (1984)

Terminator II: Judgment Day (1991)

Alien (1979)

Aliens (1986)

Back to the Future (1985)

Who Framed Roger Rabbit (1988)

FILM SCHOOL / *BOYZ N THE HOOD*

Desperately Seeking Susan (1985)

Clueless (1995)

She's Got to Have it (1986)

Do the Right Thing (1989)

Malcolm X (1992)

Chan Is Missing (1982)

Menace to Society (1993)

Shaft (2000)

Sweet Sweetback's Baadasssss Song
(1971)

Reservoir Dogs (1992)

Pulp Fiction (1994)

Blood Simple (1983)

Fargo (1996)

Look Who's Talking (1989)

The Wedding Banquet (1993)

The Joy Luck Club (1993)

Crouching Tiger, Hidden Dragon (2000)

HOLLYWOOD TODAY / *CRASH*
Spiderman (any)
Lord of the Rings (any)
Harry Potter (any)
American Beauty (1999)
Sideways (2004)

Good Night, and Good Luck (2005)
Walk the Line (2005)
Capote (2005)
Brokeback Mountain (2005)
Lost in Translation (2004)
Memento (2000)